RAISE CONFIDENT KIDS

A Parent's Guide to Raising Happy, Confident Kids

Enable EVERY child to feel
SAFE, WORTHY, AND OF VALUE

GAIL A. CASSIDY

BALBOA.PRESS
A DIVISION OF HAY HOUSE

Balboa Press books may be ordered through booksellers or by contacting:

Balboa Press
A Division of Hay House
1663 Liberty Drive
Bloomington, IN 47403
www.balboapress.com
844-682-1282

Print information available on the last page.

ISBN: 978-1-9822-5315-8 (sc)
ISBN: 978-1-9822-5316-5 (e)

Balboa Press rev. date: 09/09/2020

DEDICATION

My children, Lynne and Tom, motivated me
to be the best mother I could be
in order to match them—the perfect kids!
This book is dedicated to my family: my
husband, Tom, my two wonderful children, my
incredible daughter-in-law, Elizabeth, and
the icing on the cake, my beloved grandsons,
Patrick and Jason. You ALL bring me tremendous joy,
laughter, and love!

CONTENTS

FRAMEWORK
RAISE CONFIDENT KIDS

S - Save

A - Acceptance

V - Validation

E - Enthusiasm

S-A-V-E

C-L-A-P

C - Clap

L - Listening Skills

A - Attitude Training

P - People Skills

**UNCONDITIONAL LOVE &
BOUNDARIES**

I think tolerance and acceptance and love is something that feeds every community.

- Lady Gaga

PREFACE

People all over the world have been impacted by the Coronavirus-19 and the tragic murder of George Floyd by a rogue police officer. Finding ways to cope with the need to stay safe and the need to fight racism is daunting and is handled by everyone in their own way.

During this conflicted time, retired school teacher, Abby Foster, decided to write about what she had learned during her decades as an educator in high school settings, corporate settings, and even her two summers teaching school administrators in Lithuania. She felt that perhaps her writing could help parents deal with one of the major challenges everyone is aware of today; namely, nonacceptance of others, including racism, an extreme form of bullying. A child who does not feel acceptance from his or her peers will find it difficult to feel confident or happy.

Abby believes that everyone in the world has one thing in common, and that one thing is the desire to be happy and/or experience serenity.

The world is suffering, and yet the goodness of many people is evidenced daily in the news and on television. Today's heroes are the front-line people: doctors, nurses, custodians, cashiers, cleaners, and those who previously did not get the recognition they have now earned. Included in this mix are the peaceful protestors who believe that all people are created equal.

Abby feels that everyone at this time in modern history needs to be reminded of the ethical standards with which they were raised. She is also aware that each individual has to establish his or her own code of ethics and live by that code. Otherwise, internal conflicts arise and serenity disappears, i.e., if honesty and integrity are part of a person's code of ethics, lying and cheating would disrupt their feeling of happiness or serenity.

Abby is convinced that no one can dictate what ethics an individual should embrace. That is usually determined by individual family values, religious and ethnic backgrounds, and experiences in life. Honesty, integrity, and morality, even the Golden Rule, are usually the basics included as part of most people's values and ethics. Even if the specific ethics are not verbally spoken or discussed, they are usually the backbone of how parents raise their children and live their own lives. Abby believes that violating one's own code of ethics is what causes friction among people and among nations.

Raising a child is never easy and cannot be done perfectly. Children enter this world with their own personalities, their own uniqueness. Obviously, no one can or should attempt to tell parents how to raise their children; that is not Abby's intention. Her intention is two-fold. One is to point out the basics of human nature that we all know deep down inside but may not be aware that we know.

Her second purpose is to again tell you what you already know but may not be aware you know regarding communication skills, listening, attitude and people skills. She hopes readers will consider this a refresher course, bringing to their awareness what they already know. Having this awareness in the forefront of their minds makes it easier to share these skills with their children.

From her many years as an educator, Abby developed a Framework that is easy to remember and fits all situations dealing with other people, especially children. She encourages readers to think of a large oval frame that encompasses the most desirable basics of all human nature. Written around one side of the frame is "Unconditional Love." Around the other side of the frame is written, "Boundaries." Within the frame there are two acronyms for the easy-to-remember basics of her child-rearing recommendations: **S-A-V-E: S** (Safety, mental), **A** (Acceptance), **V** (Validation), **E** (Enthusiasm). Beneath that is **C-L-A-P: C** (Communication skills: physical and verbal), **L** (Listening Skills), **A** (Attitude Training), **P** (People Skills).

To prove that you already know this but may be unaware that you do, Abby suggests you look at anyone and then describe this person, even without speaking to them. Look at someone checking out in the grocery line. What do you see? You have an immediate impression just by the looking at someone's facial expression, posture, and tone of voice.

You may not be correct in your assessment, but you won't be too far off track. Your immediate reaction to the person you viewed is covered in Abby's Framework. Awareness is necessary in order to share what you are aware of.

The importance of bringing this information to the forefront of your mind is because you are raising a child to have internal and external confidence, a happy child who believes in him or herself.

Abby strongly believes that every child should be exposed to and master the basic academics: math, science, languages. Her experience has also shown her that a child's success in the "academics" depends on the student's inner belief about his/her own capabilities.

She recalls her eight grade math teacher, Mr Stricker, telling her that she was not capable of learning math. Because he was the adult figure, she believed him and avoided all courses that involved math. She believed she was not capable of learning anything related to numbers. It wasn't until college where she had to take a mandatory math class to graduate, that she learned she was able to learn math. In hindsight, her conclusion was the same as Henry Ford's, **"If you think you can or you think you can't, you are right."**

That personal experience with math and her observations of the students she taught, including her corporate classes, convinced Abby that the secret to successful learning is an inner belief that you can do it.

The more she observed students of all ages, whether in schools or in corporate or international settings, the more convinced she became that she could create a recipe or framework that would result in a successful school experience for those who followed it. Abby also realizes that teachers have to provide the classroom atmosphere that would allow this experience to come to fruition.

Children live up to what they believe they can do. Even adults, she believes, are limited or motivated by their own self-beliefs.

Another powerful, horribly negative impact on a child's self-esteem is bullying. Bullying negatively impacts all participants and has reached epidemic proportions, as have the number of teen suicides.

Abby's intention is to change how people view bullying by tapping into the basics of human nature and approaching those basics in a variety of perspectives in order to reinforce the importance of this message. Abby's goal is to provide a recipe or framework that enables every child to feel safe, worthy, and of value.

Her ultimate desire is to inspire parents and teachers to learn and internalize the perfect recipe or Framework for raising a bully-proofed child, one who believes in himself, will work up to his or her abilities, and can accept others for who they are. She believes that the greatest impediment to a child's confidence is bullying, i.e. non-acceptance, including physical and mental threats.

Racism is bullying; showing one's non-acceptance of another's religious or ethnic background is bullying; any personal characteristic pointed out demeaningly as different, such as color of hair, size, shape, is bullying.

No one is expected to like every person they meet, but everyone is expected to show respect. That's the minimal response for those who believe in "treating others as they would like to be treated."

In the Chapter 16 Abby goes into more detail about the specifics of bullying and what parents can do about it.

THE BASIC PREMISE
OF THIS BOOK

THE MAGIC INGREDIENT TO SUCCESS/HAPPINESS

Many years ago Abby had the honor of giving the commencement address at her local high school. She told the graduates that if she could, she would flip each of them a **MAGIC COIN** which would represent one characteristic that would positively impact their lives. She added that some students may be fortunate enough to already possess this characteristic.

This one powerful characteristic does the following:

- **INFLUENCES THE FRIENDS YOU CHOOSE** so you never have to judge others or find fault with others. You can accept others and recognize their strengths, without ever feeling threatened by their strengths,

- **DETERMINES HOW INVOLVED YOU BECOME WITH LIFE**—joining clubs, volunteering, participating on sport teams, becoming involved with town or school involvement, national involvement, activities to help others,

- **GIVES YOU INNER CONFIDENCE**—you automatically walk tall, knowing your opinion counts, knowing you can do whatever you put your mind to and be decisive,

- **HAS A DIRECT BEARING ON HOW YOU'LL LIVE YOUR LIFE**—determines your level of success in life, measured in self-satisfaction with your life.

THIS ONE CHARACTERISTIC IS CALLED SELF-ESTEEM or SELF-CONFIDENCE, and it means **"SELF-WORTH,**

SELF-RESPECT – THE FEELING OF "I'M GLAD I'M ME." It also promotes acceptance of all others regardless of race, religion, or ethnic background. No child anywhere in the world is born with a prejudice. Prejudices are learned!

YOU ALREADY HAVE SELF-ESTEEM IF:
1. You feel satisfied with what you've done so far in life
2. You **DON'T NEED TO FIND FAULT OR TALK ABOUT OTHERS**
3. **YOU CAN ACCEPT "WHAT IS'S" IN LIFE**, as in "GOD, grant me the **SERENITY** to accept the things I cannot change, **COURAGE** to change the things I can, and the **WISDOM** to know difference."

To parents, Abby added:

Every child is special in some way, and it is our job as parents to find that specialness and make sure your child knows he or she has it!

Learn how to instill this invaluable characteristic in your child or your student. It is not difficult to do, and it is fun! A child who truly believes in himself is not a spoiled child or an "entitled" child.

Having a strong self-concept allows a person to accept others as they are. People who cannot accept others usually cannot accept themselves or some aspect of themselves.

She encouraged students and parents to think about how different the world would be if everyone could see a person as she or she is, not what their race, religious or ethnic background is.

That is a goal the world should strive for, an opportunity for everyone to maximize his or her potential!

"If you think you can or you think you can't, you are right.

- Henry Ford

CHAPTER ONE

A CHILD'S CREED

Every time Abby sees a child hurting, she hurts. As a teacher, Abby has seen children in the lunchroom eating by themselves, shunned by their peers. She saw kids taunted in the hallways by the older, stronger kids–the bullies of the school. She saw kids harassed in the classroom, sometimes by their teacher. She keeps remembering the teacher who would ask students who answered the problems incorrectly to tap their foreheads ten times saying the letters "T-M" backwards which is "M-T" which equates to "empty." That recurring negative experience stuck in Abby's head.

Focusing on academic achievement for those students who have been beaten down by their personal circumstances, whether it be families, teachers, and/or peers, is secondary to focusing on the personal success they feel in life. Without a feeling of self-worth, Abby believes that most people will find personal success a challenge every step of the way.

Abby found a recent YouTube video of a cute little 3-year old walking to pre-school, laden with a large backpack and holding onto a banana while repeating the mantras his mom taught him: "I am smart!" "I am blessed!" "I can do anything!"

Abby was impressed because she believes that this is a practice that could impact his life for forever! If he believes what he says, how great will his life be!

She realized that as adults, we, too, could change our lives if we adopted and believed in this little boy's mantras. Remember, "If you think you can or you think you can't, you are right."

Believing you are smart opens doors you may have kept closed because of a fear that you aren't capable. Believing you are blessed in your current situation is choosing to see opportunities. Choosing to recognize you are okay exactly as you are, choosing to do things you never had time for, choosing to be the best person you desire to be are mindsets that could be life-changing. "I can do anything" allows us to pursue projects, subjects we may never had considered seriously, perhaps doubting our own abilities. At the age of 3, this little guy has already impacted the world. Abby loved it!

In addition to helping a child develop a positive self-concept, Abby writes about the "who" and "why" of bullying, the importance of beliefs, the role of mentoring, a basic code of ethics, the importance of nonverbal communication, listening, and tolerations, with all topics diverted back to the development of a positive self-concept in every child or student.

Abby's major concern is the effect bullying has on children– mentally, physically, and socially. The evening news broadcasts feature extremely negative examples of this hurtful behavior on a daily basis, not only in your area but across the country–even further– around the world.

She has witnessed the anti-social behavior of bullying that has morphed from pushing and calling kids names on the playground into activities that profoundly impacts lives, and in some cases, ends lives. She recalls her father's advice when she was a chid, "Just punch him in the nose if he bothers you, and he'll never bother you again." In today's society, a punch could end up in a knife fight or a shooting. Bullying can be deadly!

Abby has asked professional educators their opinion on what they believe accounts for this change in bullying? Is it what kids see on TV today, sitcoms and movies where "mean" is seen as funny or is entertaining? Is viewing bullying behavior second-hand a relief to viewers because it is someone else who is being hurt, not the viewer? Or is it TV news which shows everyday violence, and as a result, kids become inured to the pain and suffering of others, or has economics played a part? Unfortunately, an agreed upon, definitive answer does not exist.

Abby realizes that today both parents frequently work, of necessity, in order to survive, and their children frequently come home to a babysitter or sibling or no one, rather than coming home to someone who will listen and understand what's going on in their lives. She wonders if parents are more lenient in raising kids today because they are less available and want a great relationship with their kids. She doubts that parents allow "mean" behavior in their own homes.

Abby wondered if bullying has increased because of the electronic gadgets constantly affixed to the ears of kids for as many hours a day as they are allowed to listen. Are the words of songs having a hypnotic affect on the brains of our children? Are attention spans shortened, which results in having less patience with others?

Or, she further mused, is this increased bullying activity a result of the combination of ways our culture has changed? If so, what is the solution? Are there solutions? Abby believes they do exist.

She believes that solutions have to take into consideration basic human relations, basic human needs. Solutions cannot exist in a vacuum; they must have mainstream acceptance. How? By changing our culture! She believes it can be done—with everyone's help!!

Abby is certainly aware that times have changed. Technology has affected every part of our lives and mostly for the good. Even foods have changed; transportation has changed. But the one thing that has not changed is human nature. With her awareness of that one fact: human nature has not changed, Abby developed her four basic recipe ingredients, an integral part of the parenting Framework.

Whatever the reasons are for today's "lack of kindness" epidemic, Abby believes that something can be done to change the climate of acceptance of those who experience or even witness a person being picked on. To her, the most obvious, yet most difficult solution, is to shift our current culture, shift the thinking of people–everyone from students to teachers to parents–who believe that "kids will be kids" to total nonacceptance of any act of bullying. Racism is an extreme form of bullying.

Abby's ultimate goal is to get universal agreement that **BULLYING, INCLUDING RACISM, IS UNACCEPTABLE FOR EVERYONE – EVER!! Her goal is to promote a bully-free culture. She believes it can be done!!** Dorothy Nolte's "Child's Creed" shows how this can be done.

Dorothy Law Nolte was a woman who understood the field of positive youth development before it was invented. She became a parent educator, family counselor, and writer known for her inspirational poem, "Children Learn What They Live." The basics of Psych 101 are covered in this poster of "The Child's Creed":

CHILD'S CREED
CHILDREN LEARN WHAT THEY LIVE

If a child lives with criticism, he learns to condemn.
If a child lives with acceptance, he learns to love.
If a child lives with hostility, he learns to fight.
If a child lives with approval, he learns to like himself.
If a child lives with fear, he learns to be apprehensive.
If a child lives with recognition, he learns to have a goal.
If a child lives with pity, he learns to be sorry for himself.
If a child lives with fairness, he learns what justice is.
If a child lives with honesty, he learns what truth is.
If a child lives with encouragement, he learns to be confident.

If a child lives with tolerance, he learns to be patient.
If a child lives with praise, he learns to be appreciative.
If a child lives with security, he learns to have faith in himself.
If a child lives with friendliness, he learns that a world is the nice place to live.

- Dorothy Law Nolte

Abby discovered this Child's Creed hanging on the wall in her principal's office. She went online and found beautifully framed copies, even needle-point copies. Seeing it hanging on her wall every day is a great reminder for Abby.

She and her husband, Jake, have studied every line of this poem in order to make sure that criticism, hostility, fear, and pity were not practiced in their home with their children. Awareness is always step one in adopting any belief or practice. Abby knew that if she could practice this at home, she could also be a more effective classroom teacher.

EXERCISE: Make four copies of this page, and each day for four weeks put a check mark beneath the appropriate day to indicate you have read the entire poem. Remember: AWARENESS IS ALWAYS STEP ONE.

CHILD'S CREED
CHILDREN LEARN WHAT THEY LIVE

	M	T	W	TH	F	S	S
If a child lives with criticism, he learns to condemn.							
If a child lives with acceptance, he learns to love.							
If a child lives with hostility, he learns to fight.							
If a child lives with approval, he learns to like himself.							
If a child lives with fear, he learns to be apprehensive.							
If a child lives with recognition, he learns to have a goal.							
If a child lives with pity, he learns to be sorry for himself.							
If a child lives with fairness, he learns what justice is.							
If a child lives with honesty, he learns what truth is.							
If a child lives with encouragement, he learns to be confident.							
If a child lives with tolerance, he learns to be patient.							
If a child lives with praise, he learns to be appreciative.							

M T W TH F S S

If a child lives with security,
   he learns to have faith in
   himself.   _____

If a child lives with friendliness,
   he learns that a world is the
   nice place to live.   _____

- Dorothy Law Nolte

Become aware of which line or lines that you find most challenging for you.

Is there anything you would add to this Creed?

Unconditional Love
and
Boundaries
Form the Basis
of
Successful Parenting

CHAPTER TWO

UNCONDITIONAL LOVE AND BOUNDARIES

Abby thought back to their moving day when their kids were two and three years old. The moving van was almost loaded with all of their earthly belongings when the screaming of two-year old, Luke, brought Abby to a standstill. That's when she realized that the movers had put his bedroom furniture on the truck first. Unfortunately, the movers had placed his precious "blankee," the one item he never let go of when he was awake, in his dresser drawer. Washing his bedraggled comfort item took place only at night when he was sound asleep. The movers didn't know that but quickly heard about their indiscriminate placing of Luke's indispensable item.

Although the move was only a few miles from their new home and loading the van took only a few hours, Abby and Jake Foster felt as if that day lasted for an eternity because of the missing blanket.

Handling this situation of a constantly crying child was challenging. Abby believed that part of the foundation of parenting, something that comes naturally, is **unconditional love**, so that's what she did in spite of her own discomfort with this major change in her life—moving. She hugged; she cradled, she distracted, she did everything in her power to act as a replacement for his beloved comfort item.

She also strongly believed In the second foundation of parenting, the part that if not developed at a very young age would be difficult, if not impossible, to impose when the teenage years arrive; namely, **establishing boundaries**.

Crying about a missing comfort item is one thing; acting out by hitting, biting, and and kicking is another thing. Both Abby and her husband, Jake, held their ground. Reasoning would not work with a two-year old; distraction would, along with the understanding of what was acceptable behavior and what was not.

Amidst the noise and the nervousness caused by the move, Jake and Abby were finally able to get the kids strapped into their car seats and drive to their new home. They trailed behind the moving van with the kids' climbing gym attacked to the back, swaying slightly with each turn the movers made.

Packing the truck took hours; unpacking took even longer or maybe it just seemed longer with the background noise of a crying child plus another emergency that arose.

When Abby thinks back on that day, she vividly recalls the distress of her two-year old. She also recalls how she and Jake handled the problem—**unconditional love and boundaries**. Those two principles were the bedrock of their parenting.

Abby believes that unconditional love comes with the territory. Setting boundaries is a natural reaction to protect a newborn; however, setting boundaries can be a challenge every parent has to come to terms with as children grow and make more demands.

The principle of setting boundaries may feel uncomfortable. Everyone wants to be liked, and maybe the boundary will upset someone. As kids get older, they need to have input regarding the boundaries, i.e., household chores, car use, curfews, etc..

Abby was impacted by the importance of setting boundaries when she rcalls her days as a student teacher and first-year teacher. Her student teaching was divided into two assignments. The first quarter assignment went wonderfully well, and Abby was looking forward to a replication in her second quarter.

The second assignment was in a tough coal mining region of the state. Her practicum teacher was elderly and mean! As Abby observed her curt responses to the students, she, herself felt offended. Why couldn't she be nicer to the kids? It was obvious that she didn't like them, and they didn't like her.

Abby hoped she would soon be able to work with the kids. She believed that all she needed to do was be nice to them. Her wish was granted when one day an emergency arose, and the teacher was called out of the room. She asked Abby to take over.

Abby was well prepared and started the lesson in a kinder manner than her practicum teacher had ever done. She was aware the kids were paying attention, and she had no need to raise her voice or chastise any child UNTIL one boy walked to the front of the room, followed by a second boy then a third, fourth and finally all of the boys were in the front of the room and made a circle around her.

Abby's feelings of kindness turned to abject fear. All of her harshly stated reprimands to "sit down" were ignored, and for the first time ever, Abby was scared. As the boys were circling her, making the circle smaller and smaller, the classroom door opened and the teacher returned. The boys quietly moved to their seats as if nothing had happened.

Abby was was trembling from the experience, and she quickly learned that "being nice" wasn't the answer in an unfamiliar classroom. This experience taught her that she had to earn their respect before they would give it to her. She had to be the one who set the boundaries, not the kids.

The following year, at age 21, Abby got her first job as a tenth grade English teacher. Her last class of the day was on the sunny side of the building in a room that felt like a kiln. Twenty-eight boys and two girls entered the room. She learned that the average

age of these kids was 17 rather than the usual 15 years of age for sophomores.

She was greeted by catcalls and whistles as she entered the room. Remembering her terrifying experience from her last semester of practice teaching, she stopped immediately. She told the class that they had 10 seconds to be quiet when she entered the room or they would spend the period writing.

For two entire weeks, the kids wrote every day, and Abby corrected their papers every night. The positive was she learned a lot about her students through their writing; the negative was the time-consuming task of grading the papers. Nevertheless, the boundary had been set.

This was an "at risk" class of students, kids who were capable learners but were turned off and, therefore, tuned out of school. After the initial difficult two weeks, these kids gradually found a place in Abby's heart. She attributes this mutually respectful relationship to the initial setting of boundaries.

Unconditional love for her own kids was easy and was the natural consequence of being a mom. From being a teacher to becoming a parent, Abby learned that setting boundaries at every stage of the game, and in every arena, is what forms kids' expectations and what protects kids as they learn and grow.

REVIEW AND EXERCISE:

What all parents want for their children. We want them:

- To be happy and healthy
- To do well in school
- To have friends and
- To be great kids to live with and
- To feel acceptance.

FACTS:

1. **The world has changed**: technology, transportation, etc.
2. **Human nature not changed**: how people feel, act, and react

We all have the same basic needs for survival: We all need food, shelter, water, and sleep.

TWO BASIC ELEMENTS IN RAISING A CHILD:

**To be happy and successful, kids need to know they have
(1) UNCONDITIONAL LOVE from you - that's the easy part.**
(Your precious child arrives and you automatically become nurturing and protective, just as a mother lion, a mother bear is with their off-spring.)

(2) BOUNDARIES are also needed!

- **UNCONDITIONAL LOVE - EASY**

- **BOUNDARIES - DIFFICULT: This can sometimes prove to be a major challenge!**

We all want our children to love us, and what easier way to gain that love than giving them what they want.

How do you react in the following situations?

- Shopping aisle: "I want Fruit Loops!"
- Before dinner: "One cookie, please, please, please!!"
- "I don't want to wear my sweater!" In cold weather.
- "I want to talk to my friends on my phone now."
- "I want to watch one more show on TV."
- "I don't want dinner. I want my Halloween candy!" and the list can go on and on.

When do you say "NO"? Can you say "NO"?

CONSEQUENCES: If a child always gets his/her way as a young child, how can you start saying "No" in their teenage years and expect compliance? After all, they got their way whenever they begged or demanded. What's different now? **You don't want an "entitled" teenager.** Fitting in as a young adult becomes more difficult for someone who feels they should always get what they want.

UNCONDITIONAL LOVE and BOUNDARIES form the foundation for raising happy, CONFIDENT kids.

Raising children with a high level of self-esteem is vitally important in an era where bullying is on the increase. A horrifying statistic from the U.S. Secret Service is their finding that in 37 school shootings, 2/3's of the shooters had been bullied.

In addition to that solid foundation of Unconditional Love and Boundaries, there are additional actions from parents that will have a tremendous impact on their child.

Abby frequently refers to this popular quote attributed to speechmaker, Carl W. Buehner, as a measuring stick as to how well she is doing: "They make forget what you said—but they will never forget how you make them feel."

The important question to ask is "How do you make your child feel?"

Here is Abby's basic recipe for raising every child to be CONFIDENT and happy, using two easy-to-remember acronyms, one for the basic philosophy for raising a child and one for the "how-to" of raising a child.

**Raising confident, happy kids recipe: (S-A-V-E)
S - (Mental Safety) A - (Acceptance) V -
(Validation) E - (Enthusiasm)**

**How-to raise confident, happy kids: (C-L-A-P)
C - (Communication skills) L - (Listening Skills)
A - (Attitude training) P - (People Skill Training)**

Abby's challenge to parents is to master the concepts of these two easy-to-remember acronyms.

They may forget what you said — but they will never forget how you made them feel.

—Carl W. Buehner

CHAPTER THREE

PRINCIPLE #1: SAFETY

Abby had always been interested in how the mind works. In her spare time when her young children were napping, she read everything she could find regarding how people think, what motivates people, all the while trying to understand why some people are happy with their lives and others are not. Her interest was piqued even more when she read about Edgar Cayce, a self-professed clairvoyant, born in 1877 who gave 14,306 psychic readings and has over 300 books written about him. After reading numerous books on Cayce, Abby then studied Silva Mind Control, Transcendental Meditation, and EST (Erhard Seminars Training), three courses she took that made her more aware of how people see and react to the world.

The book that most influenced Abby's child-rearing beliefs was *Your Child's Self-Esteem* by Dorothy Corkhill Briggs which she read once a year, every year for five years. Reading it once was great, but some details were quickly forgotten. Reading it the following year gave Abby insights she had missed the first time. Three more readings over the next three years solidified the important messages in Abby's mind. She wanted those principles to be embedded in her mind as she raised her own kids.

As her children grew, Abby tried to find an easy-to-remember framework or recipe for raising kids, as she had found the perfect formula for baking her famous Top Me Twice cake and Bacon Cheese quiche. She used the exact same ingredients with those two recipes and got perfect results every time. She wondered if a "framework" could be applicable for raising children?

As the years passed so quickly by through tears, drama, and hugs, Abby found there were certain universal reactions everyone has - old, young, and in-between. These were the ingredients she added to her child-rearing mix.

She thought about Maslow's Hierarchy of Needs written in the 1940's and still used today as a model for human development in colleges and universities. Obviously, survival is the first step of the ladder. Abby didn't worry about her family physically surviving as she and Jake were gainfully employed and lived in a lovely home in a wonderful town.

"Safety" is Maslow's second step. Every parent worries about their children—car safety seats, helmets while bicycling, boots for the snow, admonitions such as "don't touch the stove," "look both ways before crossing the street" and so much more. Abby knew that safety was important.

Abby also recognized that there was another aspect of safety - mental safety. She was aware that young children take as gospel what their parents say to them. When they believe what they hear, they internalize the words and act accordingly.

After years of research and daily journaling, Abby believes she has found a viable, easy-to-follow recipe that every parent can adopt. The first letter of the recipe is "S" for Safety, particularly mental safety. The entire recipe is contained within the acronym S-A-V-E (**S**afety-**A**cceptance-**V**alidation-**E**nthusiasm); and that's what Abby wants to share with every parent and/or teacher.

The S-A-V-E recipe is about how you, the parent or teacher, can encourage the feelings of self-worth in anyone who doesn't have it. Abby believes that when people realize their value, they use it. If they believe they have no value, they won't because they can't.

Abby found that a major threat to the first ingredient of "Safety, particularly mental safety" is "you" messages almost every parent uses without thinking about the effects of their words on their child.

She thought of all the "you" messages she herself has uttered and has heard other parents say:
"You are such a slob! Why can't you keep your room neat?
"You are so stupid. How could you have let the dog out?"
"You're a mess? Look at the spots on your shirt."
"You really disappoint me! I showed you how to do it!"
"Can't you remember anything? I told you three times."
"You are rude! I told you to be nice to Aunt Sally!"
"You are always late!"
"You don't deserve any dinner if you can't be on time."

The list is endless. Abby realized that if kids believe what their parents say, knowing that parents are their ultimate role model, then they must be a slob, a mess, stupid, dumb, rude, undeserving if their parents told them they were.

She also realized that what was common in all of these negative statements was the word "you." What followed the "You" was what the child believed and internalized.

Abby was aware that she and Jake and most of the parents they knew frequently made "you" statements. The statement may have made sense and gotten the point across, but, she wondered if "you" statements weaken the child's foundation? "You" statements may be expedient in correcting a child's behavior, but are they the most effective ways to handle a situation?

Abby felt fortunate as she watched her kids grow. They were delightful, fun, and high achievers in their own different arenas. Their one child, however, in his teenage years constantly left wet towels on the bathroom floor, a habit that drove her husband, Jake, crazy. He complained; he threatened; he fumed until one day Abby said to him, "Drugs or towels?" He was a perfect kid who happened to leave wet towels on the bathroom floor.

23

Abby convinced Jake to switch to "I" messages rather than the condemnation of "you are such a slob!" Jake then told his son, "I really don't like seeing wet towels on the floor every day" or "I know you are busy, but I would really appreciate you hanging up your towels. This towel bar is reserved for you."

The towel caper took a while to reverse, but it did change.

Abby reminded Jake that "you" messages are habits, and habits can be changed, even if not instantly or instinctually.

As stated before, Abby came to realize that grown people are as they are a result of a number of factors: how they were raised, their ethnic and religious backgrounds, their childhood experiences, and most of all, how they believe themselves to be.

She wondered how many kids believe they are worthwhile, bright, kind, pretty, handsome, fit? She was aware that people acted according to how they viewed themselves.

Abby frequently thought about that eighth grade teacher who told her she was incapable of learning math, and she proved him right all through school until she took a mandatory math class in college and aced it. She believed him because he was the expert; she was merely a student.

Abby realized how words impact a child. She became extremely aware of "mental safety" not only as a parent but also as a teacher.

At Back to School Night at the school where Abby taught, parents usually came alone to discuss their child's progress. One set of parents came to Abby's table with their sixteen-year-old child in tow and proceeded to say negatives things about him right in front of him. Abby had this boy in her junior class and was in awe of this quiet, brilliantly creative young man who drew cartoons related to what was covered in the classroom. Abby commented on his talent, but his parents saw an underachiever and told him so regularly, and in front of Abby. The boy just stared at the floor, this young man who could draw what others could write. How did he feel when he left that meeting? What does he believe about himself?

Of course, Abby also heard wonderful stories of happy, well-adjusted kids; kids she believed will no doubt do well in life; kids who felt acceptance from their families, teachers, and peers. She felt that focusing on academic achievement would benefit those kids tremendously.

She worried about the value of focusing on academic achievement for the students who have been beaten down by their families, teachers, and/or peers. Abby felt that, without a feeling of self-worth, these kids may find personal success a challenge every step of the way.

Abby saw kids come into school early in the morning to escape the wrath of their parents or siblings. She overheard a story about a parent losing control because her son had used her expensive shampoo. One boy was locked out because he had come home late. He slept in the garage.

Because of what Abby witnessed in school, she believed even more strongly in her no-fail recipe solution for the healthy mental well-being of every child.

Mental safety-"**S**"-became one of the basic recipe ingredients Abby believed in as a part of a bedrock foundation for the formation of a child's positive self-image.

EXERCISE:

PART ONE: CHECK OFF THE PLACES OR SITUATIONS THAT HAVE PROMPTED YOU TO USE "YOU" MESSAGES, AND WRITE WHAT YOU WOULD NORMALLY SAY IN THESE SITUATIONS.

- Grocery store
- Shopping
- Playing with friends
- Visitors to your home
- Breakfast
- Lunch
- Dinner Bedtime

PART TWO: DISCUSS "I" vs. "YOU" messages with your children and ask them to monitor you.

- Make it a fun daily game.
- Post a chart on the refrigerator
- Have your child determine "I" vs. "you" occurrences
- At the end of the day, count "I's" vs. "you's"

More "I" messages are rewarded by a hug.
More "you" messages by parents recognized by a "gotcha" from your child.
Punishment for parent: Wear a rubber band on wrist and snap once for every "you" message.

"We often refuse to accept an idea merely because the tone of voice in which it has been expressed is unsympathetic to us."

–Friedrich Nietzsche

CHAPTER FOUR

"S" - SAFETY CONTINUED

Preschool years were a challenge for Abby. She loved the hours she had with her kids; she didn't like those other quiet-time hours without purpose—at least in her mind. Meals to prepare, laundry to be done, picking up and putting away were her unfulfilling answers to quiet time between naps and bedtime.

Jake was gone all day, and when he returned every evening, the entertaining part of raising kids was erased from Abby's schedule. The kids awaited his arrival as if he were Santa Claus coming home every night. They loved playing "nesting" where he was the nest and they piled on top of him. Laughter and an occasional cry could be heard from the living room where the three of them played while Abby prepared dinner.

It was during the quiet times in her children's early childhood that Abby started to formulate the four basic principles she used to raise her children, the high school students she taught as well as the corporate employees she taught.

What they all had in common is what she believes everyone feels, i.e. nobody **likes** to be wrong and/or nobody is wrong on purpose. She called this her **PRINCIPLE #1: Safety** which Abby wrote about in Chapter Three.

As mentioned previously, one major universal concern for all parents is safety: crossing the streets, falling down, playing with matches, and anything that could harm a child.

On that memorable, chaotic moving day, Abby's three-year old daughter, Lisa, sat quietly in the back seat next to her very unhappy brother who was still missing his "blankee." As they pulled up to their new home, Abby turned around to see how she was doing when she saw Lisa pop something white into her mouth. White!! The only thing white in the back seat were the mothballs in Abby's garnet bag stuffed in the space before Lisa's seat. The bag had a hole in it, and some of those poisonous round mothballs had popped out.

The day was about to become even longer. Jake quickly removed Luke from his seat while Abby frantically looked into Lisa's mouth to see if she had swallowed the mothball. She could see nothing and panicked. Her child could die; she had just swallowed poison!

With Lisa still strapped into her car seat, Abby jumped into the driver's seat and sped off to the local hospital, signed in and waited and waited and waited. Minutes seemed like hours. Abby begged for help but was told she had to wait her turn. Finally, the receptionist gave Abby the phone number of Poison Control Center. She rushed to the Emergency Room public phone and called.

Even now, Abby had to wait on "hold" until she heard the calming voice on the other end of the line The woman asked Lisa's age, sex, and coloring. She then came back and said moth balls are particularly dangerous to children, especially girls, under the age of six. Lisa was three. More panic!

The receptionist finally told Abby the doctor was ready to see them. In a curtained, partitioned examining room, the doctor examined Lisa and calmly prescribed Ipecac syrup. He didn't seem at all concerned, so Abby finally relaxed a bit.

The entire ordeal took only an hour but seemed like an eternity. Abby winced as she watched Lisa screw up her lips and finally take the syrup. Although exhausted from their move that day, Abby and Jake watched Lisa closely. Fortunately, she showed no signs of distress at all. Abby and Jake were very relieved.

Physical safety of every child is paramount and obvious. Mental safety, however, is not so obvious.

Abby is well aware of the fact that before a solution to the problem of verbally putting a child down in an attempt to make them obedient can be accepted, parents first have to have a fundamental agreement on what is important to every human being. No matter what religion, ethnic background, race, or gender, we all have certain basic needs, which, if violated, can have an adverse affect on how we experience life. Demeaning statements to children violate most of these principles and has long-term effects. That is why these verbal negative words are so dangerous to a child, physically and mentally.

During their preschool years, after the kids were in bed each night, Abby started writing about what she felt was a principle every parent and every teacher could relate to.

"S" is for Safety. Implied is physical safety. Hopefully, homes and schools are physically safe places, places where everyone's safety is assumed, including how people talk to one another. Not as obvious are "you" messages. "You" means a judgment or observation.

Abby is convinced that when a child goes to school, he doesn't expect to be physically injured. Unfortunately, in some schools that is not the situation, but in most schools, a child can expect to be physically safe.

Abby is very aware that there are exceptions to physical safety that exist. For example, she recalls Columbine, Sandy Hook and so many other schools, where large numbers of students and teachers were killed; Virginia Tech, where a student went crazy and shot over 30 people. But, again, that is not what Abby is alluding to.

As a parent, Abby believes that parents and teachers do have control over a child's mental safety. No adult wants to see a child picked on by another child, put down in the classroom by a teacher, or bullied by their peers. There is no doubt in Abby's mind that absolutely everybody wants to feel safe, and that means *no putting down, no ridiculing, no making fun of.* She strongly believes that all children have to feel safe from mental abuse.

One day at the beach, Abby saw a mother dragging her three-year old little girl by the arm across the sand, swearing at her and calling her names. Every parent has experienced moments of total exasperation, and Abby believed something had occurred that had aroused this mom's anger. From the anger she saw and the language she heard, Abby feared that this was not an unusual occurrence for this child. She wondered what long-term affects this will have on the child. Will she ever feel safe with adults? Will she believe she is as bad as her mom is telling her she is? Will she act accordingly? Will she do the same with her children sometime in the future?

Abby realized that even her fellow teachers can violate a child mentally. As mentioned earlier, she remembers the year when some of the girls in her homeroom would actually cry because of what invariably happened in their upcoming math class. This was young math teacher's class where anyone who gave an incorrect answer had to take their index finger and tap their head 10 times saying the letters T-M backwards. Abby witnessed the affect this punishment had on his students, especially the girls. That behavior violates the standard of mental safety.

Abby focused on this one principle, mental safety, which she felt was so important for every child to experience. She believes that violation of this one principle could adversely affect a child's self-image. The long-range effect is, a child lives up to his or her own inner self-image.

She also became aware of the fact that violation of mental "safety" comes in many ways.

One day Abby came into her classroom and sensed something was wrong. She heard the quiet laughter and snickers and looked around to determine the source of their attention.

There is one boy in that class who was picked on incessantly, something he frequently brought on himself. He did weird things so the kids would pay attention to him.

Psychologists say that we all want to be recognized; we often want the attention, even if it's bad attention. We want people to know that we exist. This young fellow had gotten wedgied in gym class, pushed in the hallways, and laughed at in class. His peers picked on him incessantly.

The particular day when Abby had sensed something was wrong, she looked at this boy and immediately recognized the reason for the snickering. He had cut his hair in the shape of a mushroom. Yes, a mushroom. She could see why he was being tormented. His head truly looked like a mushroom, but Abby could not allow him to be ridiculed. She even had to stifle her immediate reaction as she calmed the classroom.

This young man's desire for attention was so great that he would do anything to be noticed, good or bad. If he had someone who believed in him, perhaps his need for acceptance would be satisfied and he wouldn't continue to call unwelcome attention to himself.

Later in the class, as Abby walked around the room, she glanced over his shoulder before he could block her view, and she saw the words he had written at the beginning of his page, **"I want to kill them all."** He was supposed to be writing a holiday story.

This is a serious problem and one that Abby had to report to the guidance counselor. This bullied young man was a potential explosion."

Abby emphasized in her Journal, "S" is for safety. No laughing at, putting down, no demeaning, no verbal hurting or invalidating the person under any circumstance. She believes that if the young man with the mushroom haircut had an adult working with him, he would experience acceptance and validation which his peers have denied him. He would know he's important because a caring adult is working with him.

The personal test every parent can take regarding mental safety is becoming aware of how many times in a day you say "You......." "You" could be a positive or negative statement. If your intention is to relate something that upsets you that your child is doing, change "you" to "I" and see what a difference it makes.

As a parent and teacher, Abby believes that **corrections are appropriate and necessary; however, making a child or a student feel bad is not; verbally hurting someone is not acceptable behavior.**

At the end of one her Speaking Skills semester, Abby asked her students to write what was important to them in the class. Here are a few examples of what they wrote.

> "Because of the positive responses [the students] made the class comment on about each individual, the audience could see a complete metamorphosis in some students—students who were shy and did not have the comfort level that they had at the end of the year."

> "The reason I feel that this class is so effective to its students is because it makes you listen to someone who maybe you have never spoken to

before. It [the talks] will show sides of people that you probably think were never there. It also brings students closer together; it gives a quiet person the spotlight for just 2 minutes and it also gives the normally loud 2 minutes to be serious as C. C. showed with his talk on his father. Just by that one talk I learned a lot about all the people in the class. No one said one word or laughed once because everyone knew it was time to be serious. To see that side of someone whom I thought would never be like that in front of a class, to see how he felt good after his talk, to get some of that off his chest, to feel better about one's self was worth taking this class."

"I learned to respect others and realized that not everyone feels as comfortable as I do and that the best compliment I could give them was my full attention. I watched my peers improve and felt good about myself for being a part of it and proud of them for accomplishing their goals. I closely listened to the talks of the others in the class and learned a valuable lesson from all of them. Also, I learned that I can show many different sides of my personality and that people will still appreciate what I have to say."

Abby is a big believer in her first principle, Mental Safety. Her belief stems from her research, her years as a teacher, and her parenting of two wonderful kids.

SUMMARY AND EXERCISE: "S" - SAFETY - Mental Safety

To a child, you are all-mighty. Whatever you say, your child accepts as the truth, even if they argue with you.

Here's a test for you. Write what you say when...

- your child's room is a mess _____

  _____

- your child is late for dinner or school or ...... _____

  _____

- your child backtalks _____

  _____

- your child lies to you _____

  _____

- acts up in a public place, i.e., store, restaurant _____

  _____

Review and count how many times you began your sentence with, "I......"

How many times did you begin your sentence with "You......"

POINT:

"You" messages are frequently negative and judgmental. Remember, our words are internalized by our children. If their room is messy and we say, "You are such a pig or slob or whatever word we choose," they may come to believe, "Yes, I am a slob" and may continue to live up to those words.

If, on the other hand, a parent says, "I want you to clean up your room" or "I do not like the condition of your room" - words that do not convey a judgment. This is stating a fact, not attacking or labeling. The process of making them change is the next challenge.

These "I" and "You" messages may seem minor, but we all have to keep in mind that our child believes what we say, and if we label them, they accept our words internally, and in all probability will act accordingly.

When we think back to our childhoods, can we recall someone saying something that began with "You.." Was it a compliment, which is great, or was it a judgment?

Labeling can turn words into inner scars, words you remember for a lifetime and affects what you believe you can or cannot do in life. **YOUR WORDS COUNT!**

EXERCISE:

1. What does your child do that most annoys you?

_____

_____

_____

_____

2. What do you usually say to have your child change his/her behavior?

_____

_____

_____

_____

3. Can you see the impact of your words when you use "I" messages rather than "You" messages? How does it make you feel?

_____

_____

_____

_____

One basic human need is acceptance by someone!

CHAPTER FIVE

PRINCIPLE #2: ACCEPTANCE
S-A-V-E

Abby's recipe for raising **CONFIDENT** kids calls for the **four Basic Principles of Human Nature, four principles to which every person can relate.** Once again, her programs are based on a very simple acronym: **S-A-V-E** which stands for **S**afety, **A**cceptance, **V**alidation and **E**nthusiasm. Each letter stands for a principle that is universal, something that is applicable to every human being, something that, when applied, can enhance the possibility of each person fulfilling his/her potential.

Abby's second ingredient is **PRINCIPLE #TWO: ACCEPTANCE. Everyone wants to be accepted.**

One basic human need is **acceptance** by someone.

Abby knows that people may not care if everyone accepts them; that's not necessary, but those we admire and with whom we interact on a regular basis are important to us. For example, most people want their peers, either at work or in school, to accept them for who they are. If someone is a motorcycle rider, it may be important to him or her that their local biker group accepts them. If someone sings in the choir, they want the choir members to accept them. If they are in kindergarten, they want the other five-year olds to accept them. That's human nature.

Social isolation or non-acceptance leads to feelings of loneliness, fear of others, or negative self-esteem. Lack of acceptance can also cause conflict with the friends the socially isolated person may occasionally talk to or it cause problems with family members.

A non-accepted child may experience loneliness or low self-esteem. Over time, a person may develop social anxiety, depression, or other mental health concerns.

The one area no one wants to discuss is "suicide." Non-acceptance can lead to the feeling of "Why should I stay around?" The stories are heart-breaking and unfortunately too frequently reported.

Brain **development can be affected by non-acceptance**. Socially **isolated** children are at increased risk of health problems in adulthood. Furthermore, studies on social **isolation** have demonstrated that a lack of social relationships negatively **impacts** the **development** of the brain's structure.

Everyone feels lonely from time to time, but long periods of loneliness or social isolation can have a negative impact on your physical, mental and social health. Some signs include:

- **Physical symptoms** – aches and pains, headaches, illness or worsening of medical conditions
- **Mental health conditions** – increased risk of depression, anxiety, paranoia or panic attacks
- **Low energy** – tiredness or lack of motivation
- **Sleep problems** – difficulty getting to sleep, waking frequently or sleeping too much
- **Diet problems** – loss of appetite, sudden weight gain or loss
- **Substance use** – Increased consumption of alcohol, smoking, medications, drugs
- **Negative feelings** – feelings of worthlessness, hopelessness or thoughts about suicide

If your child experiences non-acceptance in school or amongst friends, Abby suggests that you see if you can locate the cause. The cause needs to be known before it can be corrected.

Parents must set the tone. Abby asks, "Are you accepting of your own child?"

Abby came to recognize that lack of acceptance by those we regard as important–teachers, peers, parents–is interpreted as "something's wrong with me."

She knows that no one in the world will be liked by everyone, and that's not necessary or expected. What is expected is that those who are close to a child accept them exactly as they are–skinny, fat, homely, flat-footed, shy, loud, and any of the other imperfections that could possibly be.

Abby finds so much wisdom in the serenity prayer regarding acceptance: "God, grant me the serenity to accept the things I cannot change, courage to change the things I can, and the wisdom to know the difference."

The things that you cannot change include your height, your parents, your siblings, your eye color. There are some things you can change. If you don't like your attitude, you can change it. If you don't like the grades you're getting, you can change them. What is beyond your ability to change is what you must accept as a "what is."

Acceptance means total acceptance, no matter what physical and/or mental aspects differ from the norm.

Abby learned the importance of accepting each child as he/she is. She believes that being "different" is a choice–Gothic, purple hair, exaggerated style. No judgment is needed or wanted. Their difference may be a good choice for them; it may be a bad choice, and it's okay, either way.

> A young girl in Abby's neighborhood used to use magic marker to touch up her black hair. She had light brown hair, but she dyed it raven black.

Her style was Gothic, and her boyfriend had the mohawk hairstyle which stood straight up, with a pink stripe, a green stripe, a yellow stripe. She looked different. She carried a lunch box, a child's lunch box, a little metal lunch box, sometimes Mickey Mouse, Donald Duck cartoon. That was her handbag. All through high school she did this. She was different. But, yet, when you talked to her, she had wisdom beyond her years, but if you look at her, you might make a judgment and dismiss her, which would be a total loss because she was special in her own right, bright, funny, and very artistic. She has made a living as an artist. She looks like an artist, but in high school, she stood out from the crowd and people did judge her.

Abby admired her not just because she didn't go with the flow but because she had the inner strength to be who she wanted to be. She did what pleased her. And that's okay. What works is accepting each child for who they are.

THE RELATIONSHIP BETWEEN ACCEPTANCE AND BELIEF

Abby continues to stress that "What the mind can see and believe, it can achieve." Napoleon Hill wrote his book, *Think and Grow Rich,* in the 1937, and its basic premise is still true – **"What your mind can conceive and believe, you can achieve."** You might want to be a singer, but if you can't carry a tune, you probably do not believe you can be a singer. If you're horrible in math, you're probably will not choose to be a scientist or an engineer, but you might be great in something else.

If your mind can conceive and believe in doing something, you can achieve it. According to 18th Century German philosopher,

Johann Wolfgang von Goethe, "Man is made by his belief. As he believes, so he is."

What do you believe you can do? What do you believe you cannot do?

Belief is not only pertinent to human beings, but also prevails amongst animals, even insects. For example, if you put fleas in a jar and put on a lid, they will jump up and hit their heads only a few times, but enough to realize (believe) they cannot get out. They then sit on the bottom of the jar and never try again. You can remove the lid, you can move the jar around, but the fleas will not jump again. Why? Because they believe they cannot get out.

Another example of the impact of belief is demonstrated in the training of elephants. Elephants could easily break their chains any time they desired, but they won't because their belief won't allow them to even try.

Throughout history philosophers have said that whatever you believe with conviction you can achieve. We don't want our youth to be like the poor elephant and go through life stuck because of a limiting belief that developed years ago. Help children take charge of their lives and live it to the fullest. Everyone deserves the be the best that they can be.

Dr. Herbert Benson, Director Emeritus of the Benson-Henry Institute for Mind Body Medicine at Massachusetts General Hospital (BHI), and Mind Body Professor of Medicine, Harvard Medical School, and author of numerous books, including *The Relaxation Response.* studied the effect belief had on the mind and the role it played in a person's life. Traveling to Tibet, Benson observed how spiritual men could sit on a mountain top dressed in only a loincloth covered with a sheet. As the snow fell on the sheet covering the monk, steam arose from the frozen precipitation that immediately melted. These men were capable of raising—mentally raising–their body temperatures after years of intense prayer, solitude, and practice.

Benson found that, in some tribes, the shaman or the medicine man could point to somebody after a guilty verdict in a trial and say, "Go home and die." Because of the person's belief in the powers of the medicine man, the guilty person went home and died–he believed that strongly in the shaman's words.

The point is to understand the power of belief. A child who feels he or she is not accepted comes to believe he/she is "lesser than," and that can affect everything they do in life. That is why we must remember how the power of belief is so important to remember when dealing with children.

Remember, belief is your ignition switch. You don't act unless the switch is on, e.g., the belief is in gear.

Abby found that many students who felt they were not accepted by their peers believed:

- 1) they are incapable of accomplishing something significant in school or in life,
- 2) they're not acceptable to others,
- 3) their teachers are being unfair to them, and/or
- 4) their "friends" are unkind.

Some of their beliefs might, in fact, be true; but it a parent or teacher's job to listen to them and to let them know from their perspective how they feel.

Beliefs guide behavior. Beliefs determine a person's success or lack of success in life.

Abby recommends everyone think about what beliefs they have that guide them. Ask if these beliefs are helping or hindering. If negative self-beliefs are not helping a child, parents need to develop a plan to help change those beliefs. Awareness is always the first step.

For two summers, Abby taught school administrators in Lithuania, and it was there that she became aware of another set of beliefs. Her training partner and she were there because Lithuanians had been under Russian rule for 50 years, and their education system had been decimated. Because of the treatment to which they had been subjected, many are still very tense, suspicious people twenty years later. Americans worked with them to teach them the latest ways that Americans do things in order to try to get their education system up to par. Fortunately, their schools are now just fine.

Here is where Abby learned that they had some beliefs that are different from hers. For example, there's no air-conditioning where she taught. On one hot day, Abby opened a window and opened the door to get a cross breeze. Immediately, one of the ladies got up and closed the window and another closed the door. After a few minutes of discomfort, Abby would again open the window and the door, and they would respond in a panic, "No, no, you cannot do that, because if you sit in a draft, you'll get a cold and possibly die." And they believed it. They believed if they sat in a draft, they would die.

Another belief example: when Abby first got married, her mother-in-law was horrified to learn that she washed my hair at night and went to bed with a wet head. She believed Abby would get a cold and die. She actually believed that.

Abby recommends that readers think about what beliefs they have. Jot down some of these beliefs and determine if they help or hinder you in life. An understanding within yourself will make it easier to understand the limiting beliefs of kids. What beliefs do you have about yourself, about your background? Is it positive or negative? Abby always believed her father when he said she couldn't go to college because "nice Irish girls didn't run away from home and go to college." He was wrong, but she almost let that belief keep her home.

What about your abilities? Do you believe you're good in math? Do you believe you're good in English? Do you believe you're good in science? Do you believe you're good in physical education? Can you dance; can you sing? Do you have musical abilities?

What are your beliefs about yourself physically, mentally, spiritually? These beliefs can determine how well you do in life. All you have to do is change those limiting beliefs—more easily said than done. It is helpful to have somebody point out to you what your strengths are. It's amazing when somebody hits the nail right on the head. You know it; they know it.

EXERCISE:

Abby suggests you write the beliefs you have about yourself, your background, your abilities, your future. Remember Henry Ford's quote: "If you think you can or you think you can't, you're right."

WRITE YOUR BELIEFS ABOUT YOURSELF AND LIFE:

- **PHYSICALLY:**
  - **Height**
  - **Weight**
  - **Face**
  - **Looks**

- **MENTALLY:**
  - **Learned easily**
  - **Difficulty with math, English, etc.**

- **FRIENDS:**
  - **popular,**
  - **unpopular**

- **RELIGIOUS BELIEFS?**

- **FAMILY BELIEFS?**

- **ETHNIC BELIEFS?**

- **FOLKLORE BELIEFS?**

- **MISCELLANEOUS**

STUDENT RESPONSES TO PREMISE #2: ACCEPTANCE. These were written by students after Abby's Speaking Skills class.

- "One of the major things about this course was not only talking to the class but listening to my classmates' presentations. Each person was unique in their approach."

- ". . . this is more than an academic class, but a bonding class where people learn about one another by communicating."

- "This class has also taught me how to listen to others and be able to pick out the positives."

- "... I now listen better to what people say and do when they speak.

- "This class helped me open up a lot. I became a lot more comfortable with who I am. When I talked about my parent's divorce and then seeing the support of my class, their listening and their applause made me feel a whole lot better about my speech, my situation, and myself.

  I also learned not to judge people. Through this class I learned not to think bad things about everyone else."

- ". . . the best thing I got out of this class were the friendships and connections I made. It wasn't so much at all what I learned in this class this year, but who I learned about and I guess in a small way that I may have been able to do for them."

EXERCISE: Rate from 1 (poor) to 5 (great) how you feel about each of the following areas related to your child.

- Eating habits _____
- Food choices _____
- Grooming _____
- Neatness _____
- Friends _____
- Obedience _____
- School work _____
- Cleanliness _____
- Punctuality _____
- Exercising _____
- Screen time _____
- Sibling rivalry _____
- Other _____

REMEDY: Looking at your responses, briefly write how you can help your child feel more accepted by family and friends.

STEP ONE is always accepting yourself before you can accept others.

Parenting is individual, meaning how you raise your child is often a reflection of how you have been raised, how you feel about yourself, and how you feel about how your child fits in.

Knowing and realizing that each child is different and every child is special in some way, as parents, Abby believes it is our job is to find that specialness and build on it.

- Is your child good at math?

- Does your child have a natural ability to sing, dance, play sports?
- Is your child particularly nurturing?
- Is your child naturally kind and caring?

Find what is special about your child and make sure he or she knows that you know what it is.

Validation has two steps:
(1) First comes from the outside in order to come
(2) From the inside.

CHAPTER SIX

PRINCIPLE #3: VALIDATION
S-A-V-E

Abby recognized the obvious: people want to feel special, e.g., validated for who they are. Nobody "wants" to be wrong. Notice the word "want." Abby agrees that we all are wrong at some point in our lives, but we usually aren't wrong on purpose. We make mistakes.

She found that when teaching a child, we can correct errors by acknowledging what is incorrect and helping the child understand how he/she arrived at that conclusion. Too time-consuming? Not at all. An answer of 2 plus 2 equals 5 can easily be corrected by pointing out a variable that the child included which doesn't fit, ergo, 2 plus 2 equals 4.

Years ago, Abby tried to teach this concept to a class of engineers at AT&T. They vehemently disagreed, and in their exacting, mathematical profession, she could understand why. For children just learning, however, understanding what made them come up with the wrong answer is important.

Abby would love to see every parent and every teacher implement **VALIDATION** at home and in the classroom. The basics are easy to implement; the results are potentially life-changing— **CONFIDENT** children who have a strong self-concept and can make a difference in the world.

> Abby read about Marlee Matlin, the beautiful and talented deaf actress, who was frequently on

television. She uses sign language to communicate. She can say some words, but not clearly.

She related a story in an interview about when she was 13 years old and happened to tell Henry Winkler, (the Fonz from "Happy Days") that she wanted to act. He said, "Do it and don't let anyone stand in your way."

She said, "His validation just made it all the more true and I haven't stopped thanking him since."

She is a successful actress even though she can't hear. Her success on "Dancing with the Stars" is attributable to being able to "feel" the music in spite of not being able to "hear" it.

Her real success has resulted from listening to Henry Winkler's acceptance of her disability and his encouragement and validation.

Abby found a quote from Confucius who said, "What the superior man seeks is in himself; what the small man seeks is in others."

What "validation" means is to check or provide the validity or accuracy of a person's characteristics. Abby strongly believes there is something special in everybody. Everybody! No one is put on this earth without having something special about them, and that's what Abby encourages people to find.

To Abby, validation also means "to demonstrate or support the value of." In a healthy family, a child's feelings are validated. For example, which is a more effective response from a parent to a child, "Stop crying or I'll give you something to cry about!" or "I can see you are really sad. Tell me what you are feeling."

Abby initially felt awkward using the second response because she grew up hearing the first one, but her ultimate goal was to raise children who had feelings that were validated. That does not mean validating temper tantrums or unruly behavior; those behaviors are totally unacceptable at any time.

The dictionary definition of "validation" also means "to make or declare legally valid, prove, substantiate, corroborate, verify, support, back up, bear out, lend force to, conform, justify, vindicate."

From teaching high school students, Abby observed different roles kids play: the nerds, the jocks, the brainiacs, the mallers, et cetera, and she witnessed them totally change their opinion of one another by listening to what each student said was important to them and finding that they can appreciate that person for being just who he or she is.

This acceptance came through the speaking class Abby mentioned previously, where each student would get up and talk for a couple of minutes. Upon completion of the talk, the other students had to write one positive about the talk–either the content, delivery, or impact on the audience.

At the end of the semester, one girl said that what she learned during the class was that there's something special about everyone. And that's our goal: to have parents and teachers find that something special about their child or student–that's **validation**.

STUDENT RESPONSES TO PREMISE #3: VALIDATION

- "Effective Speaking is more than a class to learn how to speak; it's a class to learn to get out of your comfort zone and let people know the real you."

- "The final and probably most important skill that I learned in class was to only look for the positive in people. Because we were instructed to write down only positive things on our evaluation cards, picking out the good in people instead of bad has become second nature to me. This skill not only makes other people feel better, but it also reflects itself on my own disposition. When a person learns to see the positive in other people it brings a much more peaceful, optimistic outlook to the rest of the world around them."

- "...The class support definitely made the class less pressuring."

- "The encouragement I received from my classmates helped me through each speech...."

- "...it helps me become stronger as a person by hearing all the positive things being said about me. ...helped me grow out of my shyness."

On Oprah's final episode of her wildly popular TV show, she highlighted the importance of validation: "I've talked to nearly 30,000 people on this show," she said, "and all 30,000 had one thing in common. They all wanted validation." Each person Oprah interviewed asked her afterwards, "How did I do?" or something similar. Each wanted validation.

"Validation" means getting feedback from others that "what I do and what I say matters to you. You hear me. You see me. You think of me. You thank me. You acknowledge my accomplishments. You appreciate my efforts."

The opposite of validation is feeling like a "nobody," feeling as if nobody cares what you want or say or do or think."

Validation can also be self-validation where you recognize your good traits and your accomplishments. So don't shy away from quietly praising yourself and let the praise you receive from others be the icing on the cake.

An extra bonus to self-praise is that you can acknowledge what you did not do. Others will be unaware that you resisted the temptation to stop for a candy bar. Or that you did not have to get the last word in when you were tempted to. Or that you restrained yourself from buying that expensive item in order to stay within your budget. But you know it. Do remember to validate what you do and what you don't do.

Validation does not **mean** you agree or approve.

Validation builds relationships and helps ease upset feelings. You need it; your child needs it.

Abby is convinced that "**No one does not need validation**" in some form.

WHY IS VALIDATION SO IMPORTANT?

Validation is key to building a strong relationship with your child. When children experience invalidation, their self-esteem decreases, as does their trust in you. Many parents, teachers and professionals in a child's life don't realize the tremendous power their words have. "You should do …." "Why didn't you…." "You should be more like…," are all roadblocks in learning and connecting with your child. Abby realized that when we practice validation skills, we show children that emotions matter and that we are here for them.

Validating means giving your child or teen the message that "Your feelings make sense. You can feel what you feel, and I am welcoming and accepting of your feelings in a non-judgmental way." Please note: validating feelings does not endorse a child's improper response to a situation,

Validating your child conveys deep empathy and helps them feel understood.

When we actively listen and show that we care, often by just being present, we are using validation. Have you ever gone to your spouse or a friend just wanting to vent and they interrupt you with "Have you tried _____?" or "You should _____." It's infuriating, right? It's likely their intentions are to help you, but they are really sending the message that your feelings aren't as important as their advice. Your children feel this way too, and it's one of the number one mistakes parents make.

HOW TO VALIDATE YOUR CHILD

1. **LISTEN.** Turn off the TV, put the phone down, or stop washing the dishes. Lean forward and show you are paying attention and fully listening. Hear them out, nod your head and ask questions.

   > In Dale Carnegie's *How to Win Friends and Influence People,* there is a chapter on listening where a little boy comes home from school and says to his mother, "I know you love me because when I talk, you stop and listen." What greater compliment is there?

2. **UNDERSTAND THEIR FEELINGS.** Repeat what you hear to see if you got it right.
   • "That must have been hard."
   • "Tell me if I've got this right: you felt hurt when the teacher chastised you in front of the other kids. What else were you feeling?"

3. **VALIDATE THEIR FEELINGS.** That does not mean you agree with their reactions, but that you understand what led to their inappropriate response. When you learn that information, you

can probe into why the teacher acted as she did. Avoid asking "why." It is accusatory and they will likely get defensive.

Your role in validation is only to listen, process and nurture. To validate is to acknowledge and accept a person. Invalidation, on the other hand, is to reject, ignore, or judge.

4. **VALIDATION IS ACKNOWLEDGMENT, NOT APPROVAL OF THEIR ACTIONS.** You can validate the feeling without approving of the action. Your child is upset. Your job is to validate the child's feelings, not their actions.

EXERCISE: Practice validating what a child does during the day. Validate positive responses such as "I really appreciate how you handled your brother when he took your toy today." See how many times you can do that in response to your child's actions each day without going overboard. You do not want your child to expect praise for every action and reaction taken during a day.

$$\frac{\text{Enthusiasm}}{\text{IS}} \atop \text{Charisma!}$$

Enthusiasm
IS
Charisma!

Charisma
IS
Enthusiasm!

CHAPTER SEVEN

PRINCIPLE #4: ENTHUSIASM
S-A-V-E

Abby particularly enjoys Principle #4 and believes it is important to add to her recipe on raising confident kids. **She considers ENTHUSIASM the flavoring or zest for her recipe.** Enthusiasm means showing excitement when dealing with a child, being genuinely interested. She found that enthusiasm is contagious. It is an attitude, and she believes we each can control our attitudes, although we may not be able to control what occurs in our lives.

Readers may think, "What if I don't feel enthusiastic?" The answer is, "Act enthusiastic and you'll be enthusiastic," says Dale Carnegie. "Fake it till you make it" has been used by Weight Watchers to encourage their members to stick to their diets. Shakespeare's quote, "Assume a virtue, if you have it not" essentially means to pretend you have the virtue; use that virtue until that virtue becomes an integral part of you.

Abby found that genuine enthusiasm is almost an assurance to your listener that your point will be positive. One of her favorite quotes is from Thomas Edison, "When a man dies, if he has passed enthusiasm along to his children, he has left them an estate of incalculable value." Emerson said, "Nothing great was ever achieved without enthusiasm." Pretend to be and you will be.

In a business newsletter, "The Pin Striped Advisor," Abby found a letter to the Pin Striped advisor asking if a person is born with charisma or can charisma be developed? The advisor responded in his column that "charisma is enthusiasm." Whether it's loud or quiet, it's a characteristic that people gravitate to, and it can be developed on one's own. Enthusiastic people are fun to be around. Abby believes that your child or student will appreciate having an enthusiastic parent.

Show genuine enthusiasm. It is contagious. Enthusiasm is an attitude, and attitudes can be controlled. While we cannot help what occurs in our lives, we can always choose our reactions.

After teaching juniors about enthusiasm in an after-school program on Kids Mentoring Kids, a young gal came up to Abby and plaintively stated, "But Miss, I can't be enthusiastic. I just can't!"

Abbey responded, "But you are, right now showing great enthusiasm!"

Perhaps a good way to describe enthusiasm to kids would be to explain enthusiasm as a combination of 1) positive mindset and 2) energy.

Some of the well-known people who have spoken about enthusiasm.

- Mark Twain said he was born excited and that is the reason for his success.

- Napoleon Hill: Enthusiasm guarantees your point will be positive.

- Years wrinkle the skin; lack of enthusiasm wrinkles the soul.

- Maxwell Maltz: You must create [enthusiasm] yourself without waiting for someone to thrust it upon you. Enthusiasm is a thought turned into a performance; it is the kinetic energy that propels you to your destination. Enthusiasm implies that you believe in yourself, that you concentrate with courage, that you practice self-discipline, that you have a dream, that you see victory in the distance.

- "People rarely succeed unless they have fun in what they are doing." - *Dale Carnegie*

- We act as though comfort and luxury were the chief requirements of life, when all that we need to make us really HAPPY is something to be ENTHUSIASTIC about.

- Enthusiasm breeds energy and if you are energetic, nothing is impossible. That is why it is said that nothing happens without enthusiasm.

- Enthusiasm is so important that somebody has said, "If you don't feel enthusiastic, then fake your enthusiasm." That is because enthusiasm is infectious and your fake enthusiasm will make others enthusiastic (they don't know that your enthusiasm is fake) and their enthusiasm will, in turn, make you enthusiastic.

When dealing with children, Abby wants you to remember, **S-A-V-E: Safety, Acceptance, Validation, Enthusiasm**. Application of these principles guarantees success when interacting with other people. Mother Teresa said, "There is that terrible hunger for love, to be wanted, to be loved, to be somebody to somebody." (The Mother Teresa Center, permission to use)

Abby's ultimate goal is not only to keep kids in school but also to have them work up to their ability. She wants to stop negative behaviors in any form in or out of school, and she wants to provide a safe mental place for kids to be in order to eliminate teen suicides.

Abby believes it is vitally important to help younger people gain confidence and self-respect. Once they have those qualities, they'll be able to do well on their own. She wants parents to think about these questions:

1. How can we get kids excited about learning?
2. How can you, the adult, prepare them to be citizens of the world?
3. How can you get them to see the value within themselves?
4. What can you do to motivate them to learn?
5. How can you provide hope and opportunity?

In your recipe box, you now have the ingredients for **S-A-V-E**, which, when applied, should help alleviate bullying and provide the atmosphere for self-esteem in every child. Abby's goal for every parent is to raise CONFIDENT, happy kids!

The definitions are simple, but not always easy. Don't be deceived; they are poignant; they are life-changing, and they require genuine **SINCERITY**–the super-glue–the absolutely necessary ingredient to effective interaction with anyone.

As simple as this formula seems, Abby encourages you to read closely, and you will find the most essential parenting tips are also there. You can see how important each aspect is!

Children need to know they are worthy and worthwhile in order for them to avoid becoming bullies or becoming a target of bullies.

The next Chapter contains a Baker's Dozen, 13 tips for parents working with their children.

EXERCISE:

1) **List the times you were aware of being enthusiastic.**
2) **What were the consequences of your enthusiasm?**
3) **List activities that encourage your kids/students to be enthusiastic.** (For example, teaching vocabulary to high school juniors was boring! Breaking them into small groups, assigning 5 words a group, and having them act out the words vastly increased vocabulary test scores, and the kids loved the assignment.)

See the invisible tattoo on every child's head that reads:
Please Make Me Feel Important!

CHAPTER EIGHT

BAKER'S DOZEN

HELP A CHILD DEVELOP A POSITIVE SELF CONCEPT

To make a child feel special, to feel valued, look at Abby's Bakers' Dozen list of tips for parents and teachers.

**PARENT/TEACHER TIPS–BAKER'S DOZEN
from "BE A FANTASTIC PARENT AND
RAISE FANTASTIC CHILDREN"**

1. See the invisible tattoo on each child's forehead that reads: **"PLEASE MAKE ME FEEL IMPORTANT."**

2. **Be (or act) enthusiastic** about everything you do. It's contagious; it carries over to your children.

3. **Accept children as they are**, and then provide the atmosphere for them to learn and love learning.

4. **Being right does not always work**, e.g.,

"Here lies the body of William Jay, who died maintaining his right of way. He was right, dead right as he sped along, but he's just as dead as if he were wrong."

5. **Know that children "mirror" you.** They reflect what they see, hear, and feel from you.

6. **Show respect to get respect.**

7. **Help children to recognize their specialness.**

8. **SMILE**. It warms a home.

9. **Everyone desperately wants to feel special.**

10. Make **SINCERITY** your No. 1 priority.

11. Get children involved with family chores. **Teaching responsibility must begin early**.

12. Know, you **cannot <u>NOT</u> communicate.**

13. Remember, people have two basic needs: they need to know that they are **lovable** and **worthwhile**.

Abby feels strongly about each one of these basic principles; they are so important and so easy to implement.

SUMMARY: Give kids unconditional love and well-defined boundaries, mix it up with the 13 tips, and you will have a child steeled against bullying and also imbued with a positive self-concept, i.e., a CONFIDENT, happy child.

EXERCISE: Teach kids a memory device that will allow them to remember all 13 tips. Each word in bold represents one of the 13 tips. Encourage the kids to visualize the bold set of words before the pictures are explained:

Tattoo, Cheerleader, Infant, Speeding Car, Mirror, Saluting, Special Cane, Cheshire Cat, Gold Star, Insurance Policy, Dog Lease, Dog Licking Your Face, Lovable and Worthwhile.

1. See the (1) **TATTOO** on the forehead of the (2) **CHEERLEADER** who is holding an (3) **INFANT** as she gets into a (4) **SPEEDING CAR**. She sees in the (5) **MIRROR** of the car someone (6) **SALUTING**, holding a (7) **SPECIAL CANE** in his other hand along with a (8) **CHESHIRE CAT** who has on his collar a (9) **GOLD STAR** to which is pinned an (10) **INSURANCE**

POLICY along with a (11) **DOG LEASH** which is attached to a playful (12) **DOG LICKING YOUR FACE**, showing how (13) **LOVABLE and WORTHWHILE** he thinks you are.

2. Ask for a volunteer to recite the picture to you, then another. Ask for a third volunteer but ask him to recite it backwards.
3. Once you feel they all have the picture in their heads, then go back and relate each picture to a Tip.
4. Finally, ask someone to recite the picture and the tip represented in the picture. Once everyone can do it, you will know that they "got" it! The Tips now belong to them.

Go back to the Baker's Dozen and relate each bold-typed word to one of the dozen tips. Ask a student to recite all 13 tips without looking, using only the list of words. Then ask someone to do it backwards.

FRAMEWORK
RAISE CONFIDENT KIDS

S-A-V-E

C-L-A-P

UNCONDITIONAL LOVE & BOUNDARIES

CHAPTER NINE

S-A-V-E SUMMARY

The four Basic Principles (ingredients) of Human Nature are as follows:

S - SAFETY: Mental safety implies no verbal insults or invalidation of any kind.

A - ACCEPTANCE: Total acceptance by friends, parents, and teachers is necessary in order to for a child to experience self-worth.

V - VALIDATION: Everyone has something special about themselves. Find that specialness and make sure the child knows what it is.

E - ENTHUSIASM: Enthusiasm means showing excitement when dealing with a child. Modeled by an adult, a child learns this positive attitude.

EXERCISE FOR TEACHERS:
1. Ask your child or your class to write at least three words that they find hurtful.
2. Next to each word, write a brief sentence telling what happened to make this word hurtful to them.
3. In a classroom, pair off in twos and discuss each word between each pair. Each student gets 3 minutes to talk, then switch.
4. In each pair, have the receiver tell why the words hurt. Have class members respond to the words to see how many feel the same way.

OBJECTIVES:
- To have children not internalize the words.
- To be able to develop immunity to these words.
- To increase their confidence.

EXERCISE FOR PARENTS:
1. Take one page and divide it into three columns.
2. In Column One, list the annoying behaviors your child exhibits.
3. In Column Two, next to each behavior, write how you handle the situation when it arises.
4. Check your responses and see if you exhibit any behavior that is not in accordance with the S-A-V-E principles.
5. In a third column, write how you could handle the situation in an effective manner using the principles of S-A-V-E.

OBJECTIVE:
• To increase your own self-awareness in accordance with the S-A-V-E principles and the Child's Creed recommendations.

WHY IS MASTERING "S-A-V-E" SO IMPORTANT

All kids want to be loved, to be wanted, and to be somebody to somebody."

Remember **S-A-V-E**: **Safety, Acceptance, Validation, Enthusiasm**. In these words are the secrets of success in whatever you do dealing with other people, all people, not just those you are raising.

The bottom line is we want our kids to be happy, to be accepted, and to do well in school. We want confident kids! We do not want discrimination of any form to occur.

We want to maximize every child's self-esteem, and we want to provide a safe mental place for kids to be in order for them to maximize their potential.

Now you know the "why" of S-A-V-E - why it is so vitally important to help our children gain confidence and self-respect as a result of your reactions to them. Once they experience "acceptance" and "validation," they will be able to do well on their own.

In the next section, Abby shows you how these six steps are implemented with another acronym: **C-L-A-P**.

Following is a **Daily Check Sheet** page where you can check off daily how well you have mastered the five areas, Have fun with this, and see if you notice a difference in your child. List 5 challenges you would like to change in each of the following areas:

DAILY CHECK SHEET
In each box, note areas you feel you need to work on.
PRACTICE MAKES PERFECT!

	BOUNDARIES	SAFE-MENTAL
Mon		
Tues		
Wed		
Thur		
Fri		
Sat		
Sun		

	ACCEPTANCE	VALIDATION	ENTHUSIASM
Mon			
Tues			
Wed			
Thur			
Fri			
Sat			
Sun			

PART TWO

REMEDIES

C-L-A-P

Body language and tone of voice - not words - are our most powerful assessment tools.

- Christopher Voss

CHAPTER TEN

COMMUNICATION
C-L-A-P

Abby finds communication skills fascinating and fun. She recognizes that nonverbal communication problems arise because we cannot **NOT** communicate. You cannot **NOT** communicate. By not responding, you're communicating. By staring ahead, you're communicating. The grimace, the frown, the happiness–it's all communication. You cannot **NOT** communicate.

The second communication problem is we don't all see things in the same way. We can look at the same object and see something different according to what draws our attention. As part of one of Abby's courses in graduate school, she was assigned to sit with a classmate, looking straight ahead and free-write for 20 minutes. When she and her partner finished, she was astonished that what her partner had written about, Abby had never noticed. They were both staring straight ahead. The vista was identical, yet her partner wrote about the ship straight ahead and its maintenance, while Abby wrote about the distant trees across the water and the sandy beaches in front of us. They both looked at the same thing and saw something very different.

Albert Mehrabian's research in the 1940's is the source of nonverbal communication statistics that experts use today. His formula for how we read people is divided into three parts: 55%, 38%, and 7%.

Fifty-five percent of the message that you get when you encounter somebody is by what you see when you look at a person, e.g. their body. An example of how strong nonverbal communication is, think about a time when you went home and recognized immediately that the person you live with is very angry and they had not uttered one word. How could you tell? Abby believes that you can tell immediately because of their body language. They could be holding their bodies in a stiff manner or look at you in a strange manner, and you know by looking if they're annoyed or if they're happy.

Thirty-eight percent of the message comes from your voice– the tone, the pitch, the speed, the intensity. Tone, pitch, rate of speech are all part of the message. For example, if Abby says, "Nice tie," is that a compliment? The words are okay, it is a nice tie, but the tone may tell you that she is making fun of it, and you know that already. As mentioned, the largest percentage of the message comes from body language. The problem is what we see may not be what is.

BODY LANGUAGE:

> For example, there's the story about two men walking across a field when they feel the ground shake. They turn around and see a bull bearing down on them.
>
> One friend runs to the closest tree, throws his legs around the branch and pulls himself up. His friend runs down the hill with the bull getting closer and closer. All of a sudden, the man disappeared–there was a cave at the bottom of the hill.
>
> The man in the tree watched and suddenly his friend came out of the cave. The bull attacked again, and he ran back in.
>
> A few minutes later, he came out again. The bull attacked, and he ran back in.

This continued for quite some time. Man out, bull attacks, man in. His friend couldn't understand. Finally, the bull got tired and walked away up over the hill. The friend climbed down from the tree and met up with his friend at the cave entrance and asked, "Why didn't you stay in the cave?"

His friend responded, "I couldn't, there was a bear in the cave!"

The point is what you see may not be what you think. If a friend fails to say hello or sounds brusque when you see them, remember, he or she could have come from a place where there was a bear in the cave.

There is also a fun and true story about Clyde Von Olson and his talking horse.

At the turn of the century, there was a Herr Von Olson who trained this horse, Hans, to do simple arithmetic by tapping his front hoof in answer to a math question.

Such was the animal's prodigious ability that its fame spread quickly throughout Europe. Contemporary reports suggest it was an intriguing and baffling act. Not only could clever Hans perform addition, subtraction, multiplication and division, he was also able to solve problems containing fractions and factors.

Without Von Olson uttering a word, Hans could count out the size of the audience or tap the number wearing hats or glasses or respond to any other counting question asked.

Hans quickly attracted the attention of scientists. A commission was set up to establish whether this was a case of clever trickery or equine genius. Hans performed before professors of psychology and physiology, a circus owner, vets, Calvary officers.

Von Olson was banished from the room, but Hans was still able to provide the right answers with apparent ease. The commission announced itself satisfied that the horse really could understand arithmetic.

But a second, rather more perceptive board of inquiry put an end to that belief. They asked the horse questions to which no single member of the audience knew the answer. For instance, Von Olson was asked to whisper a number into the animal's right ear while another member of the audience whispered a second number into his left ear. Under these conditions, Hans remained dumb.

The explanation was simple. Hans wasn't especially bright, but he was very observant and highly skilled at reading human body language.

When Hans started to answer a question, the audience became tense. It was only a slight increase in arousal, too slight for the human eye to detect, but perfectly noticeable to the horse. Then, when the correct number of hoof beats had been tapped out, they would relax again. Hans noticed the change in nonverbal behavior and stopped tapping.

"His cleverness," remarked Dr. Von Knapp, "was not in his ability to verbalize or understand verbal commands, but in his ability to respond to almost imperceptible and unconscious movements on the part of those surrounding him."

We humans do the same. We detect the change in someone's body language, even though we may not be aware of it.

NODDING:

Did you ever notice that when you're talking, you tend to nod your head to make a point? In the future, be aware of your listeners. You'll notice that they, too, nod their heads when you're speaking which is their way of validating what you say. Abby mentions this here because when you're working with a child, you might notice as you're talking, he or she is nodding. If they're not, then you have to communicate in a different manner to get them on board with you.

PHYSICAL RAPPORT:

One solution is to establish physical rapport with a child. Assume the body position of the person you are addressing establishes rapport, i.e., copy their posture. The person, your child, student, spouse, will be unaware you are duplicating their posture, arm and head positions, but they will feel more comfortable.

Step one in Cognitive Coaching, a relatively new type of coaching for teachers, stresses the importance of establishing rapport through imitating the listener's body.

EYE MOVEMENT:

Also, when you're talking to someone one-on-one, you'll notice their eyes will look at your face in a definite manner; namely, eye to eye to nose and back again. During an interview, the interviewer's eyes generally go from eye to eye to nose. This is done unconsciously; no one thinks about it. But if you start feeling uncomfortable as you're being interviewed, notice the interviewer's eyes. He may go eye to eye to mouth, maybe to chin, that's almost a flirtation, and it's not something that you want to have happen. This information is the result of studies done where cameras are recording all of the actions of both the interviewer and the interviewee.

Be aware of how someone is looking at you; notice where their eyes are directed.

EYEBROW FLASH:
An unconscious nonverbal response when you see a friend is having your eyebrows automatically go up. It's called an eyebrow flash. However, notice what happens when you see somebody who catches your eye. Your eyebrows stay up a little bit longer. It's unconscious. It's not something that you think about. It's just something you do. When you become more aware of body language and what it means, you can adapt to make a better impact on whomever you desire.

Abby read a story about two men who were arrested for robbery and were interrogated separately. Each swore he did not know the other person. On their way to their cells, the two men passed in the hallway. They did not acknowledge one another but they both did an unconscious eyebrow flash which indicated to the guards that they did know one another.

SPACING:
The spacing between people is also subconscious. When you stand talking to somebody, you're usually about 18 inches apart. If they move closer, you start to feel uncomfortable. In some countries, the custom is to move closer. In the Mideast, you'll see men talking to each other eye to eye with their toes just about touching. In the United States, it's uncomfortable to have somebody stand in your space. An 18-inch separation is the norm in the United States. If you have somebody from another country, they, via their own customs, stand closer when they're talking. And you just have to adjust to make yourself feel comfortable.

HANDSHAKE:

A strong body language message is conveyed and an impression made by the way you shake hands with someone.

If you shake a person's hand, you could be demonstrating a firm handshake, which connotes confidence. If you have a limp, dead fish handshake, lack of confidence is conveyed, perhaps read as "you aren't as strong."

Sometimes you'll have someone shake your hand in a very active pump-handle shake or a delicate fingertip shake or a bruiser, bone-crusher shake, and you will interpret that also.

What you want to aim for is a confident shake. It gives the impression that you want to make, one of confidence. If you're shaking your child's or student's hand, shake with confidence. If they don't shake with confidence in return, ask them to shake again because you're the one who is guiding them; you're the one who's making a difference in their lives.

VOICE:

Thirty-eight percent of the message is conveyed through the voice, through the tone, pitch, speed, and loudness.

> One story that demonstrates the value of voice use is the story about Mark Twain who was known for his salty language. He swore like a sailor.
>
> One day, he was getting dressed and reached into his closet for a shirt. As he put it on, the button popped off, and he swore.
>
> He took out the next one and found a broken button. He threw it on the bed and swore again.
>
> He took out the last shirt and found it was totally missing a button. He slammed the shirt onto the

93

bed and swore like a sailor. He used every foul word he knew. What stopped him was seeing his sweet wife standing in the doorway with her hands on her hips and looking very upset.

In order to teach him a lesson, she walked into the middle of the room and repeated every single foul word he spoke. When she finished, she turned and saw him leaning against the doorjamb with a twinkle in his eye as he said,

"You've got the words, but you don't have the music."

The point is when you hear somebody swear, it's usually with anger behind the words. If you were to swear and it doesn't convey anger or disgust, it's not the same thing. If you were to use the word *spaghetti*, you could make it into a foul word by saying in an angry voice, "What the spaghetti do you want to do?" You know what's intended just from the tone of the voice, from the pitch of the voice, from the way the words are spoken.

Again, if you say, "Nice tie, guy," you may not be complimenting; you may be making fun of the tie. It's all in the tone of voice. If your mother ever says to you, "I don't like that tone of voice" and you say, "All I said was …" and you repeat what you said, the words might be fine, it's the tone that goes with the words that really is the message that you're trying to convey. If you were to say, "Get out of here," you could say it in a way to express disbelief. You could mean the words. You could laugh and say it as an absurdity.

Think about "Good morning." How many different ways can you say *Good Morning*? There are dozens of ways to say it. Why does that make matter? People respond to your tone of voice more strongly than they do to your words. If you say *Good Morning* in a lively manner, they're going to feel welcomed. If you say *Good Morning*, with disgust in your voice, they will not feel welcomed.

It's not the words spoken that matter, it is the way they were spoken.

How may interpretations of this sentence can there be? "I didn't say she stole his wallet." There are seven words, and there are seven possible definitions.

- Definition #1: *I* didn't say, (meaning it was Margaret who said it.)
- Definition #2: I *didn't*, (now you're denying.)
- Definition #3: I didn't <u>say</u>, (I really "wrote" it in a letter.)
- Definition #4: I didn't *say* <u>she</u>, (I meant her.)
- Definition #5: I didn't say she *stole*, (she just "borrowed.")
- Definition #6: I didn't say she stole *his*, (it was really hers.)
- Definition #5: I didn't say she stole his *wallet;* (it was really she just borrowed his wallet.)

The emphasis on each word gives the entire sentence a different meaning. You know that and you use it automatically. Abby brings it to your awareness only because you want to be aware of how your child or student is feeling when you're speaking to them.

WORDS:
Seven percent of the message comes from the words.
Describe a duck that's ready to eat. Some of you will describe the duck as "white," as you picture a beautiful swan, ready to eat the food on the pond. Some of you, however, might say "golden brown," as you picture your bird being roasted for turkey dinner, and you would be right. If you chose white and you are thinking of a duck on a pond, you are right. **The point is your language must be clear.**

On a humorous note, husband bought his wife a parakeet from a pet store. She wanted a canary, so, the next day, she went back to the pet store and said. "I'd like to exchange this parakeet for my husband." The pet store owner said, "We don't trade husbands."

Chuckle, chuckle. Just be aware of language; be aware of what interpretation your words could have.

Stephen Covey's highly recommends that each of us take the time to understand rather than be understood. Our senses, our observation, and the words we hear combine to allow us to better understand the person speaking.

Another example of verbal lack of clarity is found in the following Steven Covey story.

> Another story from Steven Covey's <u>Seven Habits of Highly-Effective People</u> talks about an adventure in the North Seas.
>
> Shortly after dark, the lookout on the wing of a bridge reported, "Light bearing on starboard bow." This was a training squadron that had been on at sea in maneuvers in heavy weather for several days, and this fellow was serving on the lead battleship and was on watch on the bridge as night fell. The visibility was poor with patchy fog. The captain remained on the bridge, casting his eyes in all directions.
>
> When the lookout said shortly after dark, "Light bearing on the starboard bow." "Is it moving or steady?" The captain called out. The lookout responded, "Steady, Captain," which meant we were on a dangerous collision course with that ship.
>
> The captain then called to the signalman, "Signal that ship, we are on a collision course, advise, you change course 20 degrees." Back came a signal, "Advisable for you to change course 20 degrees."

96

The captain said send, "I'm a captain, change course 20 degrees."

"I'm a seamen second class," came the reply, "You had better change course 20 degrees."

By this time, the captain was furious. He spat out, "Send, I'm a battleship, change course 20 degrees."

Back came the flashing light, "I'm a lighthouse," and we changed course.

The point is, take the time to understand rather than be understood. If you're making a point with your child or student, listen carefully to see as well as hear what she is really saying. He or she might be on the same page with you and they might not be. Just remember, "God, grant me the serenity to accept the things I cannot change, courage to change the things I can, and the wisdom to know the difference."

It is worth stressing again that when working with your children, the number one priority is to make sure that sincerity is your number one priority.

EXERCISE: On index cards or post-it notes, write one word on each card: DISGUSTED, SCARED, DEMANDING, BORED, SHY, SAD, CONFIDENT, HAPPY, LOVING, ANGRY, DISAPPOINTED, COULD CARE LESS, SUPERIOR, HURT, plus any additional emotions you can think of.

Assign your child or a student to each card and have them silently demonstrate the emotion in front of the room and have their peers interpret the emotion.

ANOTHER EXERCISE: Have students assume different body positions and have classmates interpret the meaning:

Shrugging shoulders, hands on hips, arms crossed, pointing index finger, head titled to one side, palm of hand held to cheek, clenched fists, slipped shoulders, shoulders back, pacing, and any additional positions you can think of.

Listening is the greatest compliment you can pay another person!

CHAPTER ELEVEN

LISTENING
C-L-A-P

Listening is the least studied aspect of communication. As Abby says, we all do it, but we don't all do it effectively. How many people know how to become an effective listener? Listening is one form of communication that is rarely covered as a form of communication; how to speak well is, but not how to listen well.

The first step is to effectively utilize silence. After you have asked someone a question, just be silent. Say nothing until you hear a response. Don't try to fill the gap of silence with your words. This is a tactic used by reporters as they interview celebrities. Notice they'll ask a question, and if the celebrity doesn't respond, there's silence. The celebrity is going to respond because silence is deafening; it's too loud.

Step two is to avoid thinking about what you're going to say while waiting for or listening to a response. Pause before you respond.

The third step is to hear the words spoken as well as those not spoken. Hear not only the words, but also the tone, the inflection, the rate of speed, the energy, the emotion that come with the words.

The words may be positive, e.g., "Nice shoes;" however, the voice inflection might indicate ridicule of the shoes. As we said in the last session, the message comes not from the words; it comes 38 percent from the voice, the inflection, the tone; and even more,

55 percent from the body language that accompanies the words. Hear the words spoken and those not spoken.

Step Four is to listen with your senses. When you feel that the words you are hearing contain more than the message, question the speaker to see if he or she is willing to reveal more than he or she has said. Strengthen your inner hearing skills. The more you consciously practice these steps, the more proficient you become in your communication skills.

Initially, you might not be comfortable as you become aware of the steps to effective listening because listening is something you've done all of your life, and you've never been aware that you are or you are not listening.

On the other hand, when you feel you are not being heard, you might even say to somebody, "Well, I know you hear me, but have you listened to me? You might hear my words, but have you listened to me?"

Years ago, in Abby's town, two schools were closed, and the parents were furious. They attended board meetings equipped with statistics and facts to justify their position. After many meetings, one parent said in exasperation, "You say you are listening, but you definitely are not hearing us!"

One way to show that you are listening to another person is to **reflect back what you hear.** In other words, paraphrase what you have heard, for example, "You believe you were treated poorly," even if the words did not say that directly. The speaker will either confirm or deny your interpretation. Reflecting back what you hear is a great way to clarify communication.

Step Five is to get further clarification when working with your child or student. Seek additional information in three areas: What happened? How are you feeling? What do you want? Don't move on until you're satisfied with the response.

Step Six is to get your child or student to say more, using words and phrases such as, "Really?" "Are you sure?" "Tell me more." "That's very interesting." "Keep going."

Keep the child on track. "I'd like to hear more about ..." One way to stay on track is not to interject too much, even though you might want to. What you want to listen for is the authenticity and truth in what they are saying. Listen for tone and language.

Does the child or student really mean what he or she is saying? What is really talking through them? Themselves? The past? Their needs? Their fears? Love? Parents? Friends?

Abby is aware that when any one of us speaks, we may not purposefully mislead somebody, but we want to maintain the façade of somebody who's not bothered by whatever is going on in our lives, and here is where the tone and the body language will tell you even more than the words. Listen for their true desires, listen for progress and their level of commitment to what they are doing and to their goals. Do they know what they really want?

If you were to say to almost anyone, "Do you know what you want in life?" you may not get a true answer; you may hear what the person is thinking at the time. Why? Most of us don't know the answer to that question. If you are an accomplished singer, you probably know you want to be a singer, but most of us don't know with clarity what we want in life. Whatever response you get from your child or student, listen carefully, watch his body, listen to her tone of voice.

Listen for fear. Listen for concerns; listen for words indicating less than desirable behaviors and blocks. Through questioning, find the source of their fears and help them overcome them. We all have fears, and frequently it is fear that blocks us from getting what we want in life. Fear embraces a number of areas: fear of being embarrassed, fear of failing, fear of not being capable.

103

Listen for support. Are they missing personal support? Are there personal or school subjects where more support could be given? Who can provide that help for them?

Listen for positives. When possible, find the positives in their lives and focus on them. Stress what's good in their lives. If they start focusing more on that, perhaps more good will come.

Point out progress and/or growth. Listen for your own reactions to the person speaking, whether it is your child or your student. How are you reacting? How is your reaction affecting your relationship? Point out to your child or student specific ways in which you are developing as a result of this relationship. What a compliment to the child if they feel that you are benefiting as a result of working with him!

To repeat, listen for authenticity and truth via tone and language; listen to their true desires, their fears, the support they may have or not have, the positives in their lives, and your own reactions.

After carefully listening to your kids, the greatest gift you can give them is the incentive to take responsibility for their thoughts and actions. "Change your thoughts and you change your world" has been recommended by psychologist, William James.

That statement seems so simple, yet it is so true. Everyone has control of how they think. Thoughts pop into your mind, but if you're focusing on something negative, negativity will appear. If you focus on the positive, more positive things will appear in your life. You already know people who see the world in a positive light, and you know people who always see the negative. How do you see the world? And how is that reflected in your child or student?

"Responsibility is as responsibility does." Taking responsibility for yourself is the goal you want your kids to have.

According to Winston Churchill, "The price of greatness is responsibility."

Abraham Lincoln said, "You cannot escape the responsibility of tomorrow by evading it today."

"Today, more than ever before, life must be characterized by a sense of Universal responsibility, not only nation-to-nation and human-to-human, but also human to other forms of life." - Dalai Lama

EXERCISE: Challenge yourself to emulate 100% of the look, stance, arm placement, of the person talking to you.

Try this exercise with at least five people and write down what you notice that is different from previous conversations.

"Change Your Thoughts and You Change Your World."

- William James

CHAPTER TWELVE

ATTITUDE TRAINING
C-L-A-P

A few years ago, Abby had the opportunity to train an entire transportation department in a small, one square-mile city, outside a large metropolitan city. These were the men and women who gave out tickets or attached bumpers to cars in order to have them towed away. Each was in a position to do what had to be done in order to keep the city safe, and their rewards included being cursed at, pushed, even having foul substances thrown on them. Obviously, no one ever thanked them for the ticket they received.

Abby started the training by showing them the results of a study indicating the importance attitude plays in a business situation.

Years ago, the Chicago Board of Trade did a study on why people change their place of business and came up with surprising statistics: 1% died; 3% moved; 12% word-of-mouth from friends; 9% price; 14% inferior merchandize; and **61% because of the attitude of the person waiting on them.** The point is, "You keep your positive attitude when you give it away."

Her job was to teach them how to control their attitudes in the trying situations they found themselves daily. First, she had to clarify what attitude is and how it can be controlled.

What exactly is attitude? Attitude is how you see the world, what you think about the work and/or how you feel about the world. **The positive is you always have control of your attitude.** You may not be able to control what happens to you, but you can control how you react.

Before her classes met for the first time, Abby sent each participant a questionnaire to find what was most bothersome to the them and to let them know what to expect from the program.

On the day of training, each received a letter she wrote: "Thank you so much for being here today and participating in our seminar training.

"From reading your responses to the questions on the Questionnaire given to each of you, I have a better understanding of some of the challenges you face every day. Hopefully, by the end of this session, you find ways to handle many of the situations in a manner you prefer.

"I believe it is safe to say that we all want to feel as if we are making a difference in the world, no matter how great or small; and that sense of making a difference makes us feel good.

"By the end of our class, I hope you will be able to judge whether or not my objectives have been met. They are as follows:

- To learn how to improve relationships among co-workers and clients/customers.
- To learn how to choose and change your attitude whenever you decide to do so.
- To learn to recognize and effectively use non-verbal communication signals.
- To master nine human relation skills.

"Hopefully, you will find this session fun and informative, and I hope you will be able to use what you learn in your daily routine in order to make your day more pleasurable.

"There is nobody who does not want to feel good every day, all day. Obviously, other people may challenge you on a daily basis. My personal objective is to recognize I cannot help what happens to me during the day, but I can be in charge of how I react to any person and/or situation.

"My challenge to you is to make your job on a daily basis as positive as it possibly can be."

She stressed that **ATTITUDE IS THE KEY TO SUCCESS,** the same words she emphasized to her kids and her students. "Everything can be taken from a man but one thing: the last of the human freedoms—to choose one's attitude in any given set of circumstances" – Viktor E. Frankl. A very simple but true statement.

The only thing you can't take away from me is the way I choose to respond to what you do to me. The last of the human freedoms is the power to choose one's attitude in any given circumstance and seemingly hopeless environment. The important question is, "What is attitude?"

Years ago, Zig Ziglar was known for his basic belief, "It is your attitude, more than your aptitude, that will determine your altitude."

The phrase "**Your Attitude determines your Altitude**" **is** a catchy double-entendre. It **means** two things to Abby: 1) What you think about yourself and **your** prospects in life, i.e. "**attitude**" dictates (2) **your** level of success, i.e. your "**altitude**".

In life, attitude is everything. Check the people around you and observe their attitude barometer - negative or positive - and if the results are negative, then you may need to look at your own attitude and make certain adjustments. Usually people mirror their own unconscious feelings and attitudes about life that they perhaps are not acknowledging head on. Remember, attitude determines a person's success in life. That's why it's so important to be choosy about those people we do spend our time with.

People become what they think about, and who they surround themselves with every day strongly influences what they think about or become.

A positive attitude is not about displaying a phony smile, a happy face and a perky disposition. It is simply a way of responding to life in a manner that allows us to accept the duality, the contradictions, the contrasts of our experiences.

A positive attitude enables a person to make a difference in the world around them because when they are able to see things in a positive light, they help to influence and shape other people's attitude as well.

Again, attitude is the mental state or position people take regarding their lives and affairs. This means it is not what they think but how they think it.

Abby stressed that a person's attitude forms every event in their life, whether they realize it or not. Out of a person's attitude comes their enjoyment of life and gratitude for all of their blessings.

Out of their attitude also comes their disappointment and anger at how things have turned out.

Out of a negative attitude comes the feeling that no accomplishment will be ever be good enough or that they are not good enough. Everyday, a person's attitude is challenged by other people and by external factors. How will they react? Will they allow adversity to stop them from moving forward? Will they allow a negative person to ruin their day, make them lose their cool, or force them to give up on their dreams?

Abby recommends that when such temptations come knocking on your door, stand at the door of your mind and declare powerfully and silently, "No one is home." In other words, don't engage.

A negative **attitude** is almost a guarantee that **life** will be more difficult and less fulfilling than it should be. Further, a pessimistic outlook will adversely **affect your** health, relationships, and professional growth.

The awareness of being willing and able to control attitude accidentally happened years ago when Abby's children were in high school. Abby had a PTO meeting scheduled for 7 p.m. one evening in her home, so she made sure everything was neat and clean before she left for work the morning of the meeting. She arrived home at 6 and found her house in shambles. There were potato chips on the floor, rings on the table, pillows flattened, furniture in disarray, and she went bonkers. Her daughter had had a team meeting after school, and the kids had just left.

Abby was beside herself. "How could be so inconsiderate!" And she ranted on. The phone rang and Abby picked up and said, "Hello!" In her sweetest voice.

When she hung up, her daughter said, "How could you do that? How could you switch from being so mad and then be so sweet?"

The question was well deserved, and it made the point that attitude is indeed controllable. From that time forward, Abby was motivated to learn more about attitude, how to control it, and what personal effect it has on each individual.

There was a study at the University of California Medical School where people had electrodes attached to them, similar to a polygraph test, that measured their heart rate, galvanic skin response, and other physiologically measurable parts of the body.

When the experiment began, they were seated in a place where suddenly a bear attacked them—obviously a simulated bear. Then they were asked to imitate the posture and intensity of feeling they had when the fake bear attacked them. The responses were almost identical.

The point is, each one of us can control our feelings a lot more than we think we can.

EXERCISE: Everyone stand and notice the different feelings you have when you assume the positions that you think represents each of the following:

- **Look confident.** How does that look? Shoulders back, head up.
- **Look insecure.** How does that look? Did your body shrink into itself? Shoulders slump?
- **Look happy.** Is your body now more relaxed? How does this feel?
- **Look depressed**. Again, did your body shrink into itself?

The point Abby was making to her beleaguered transportation students was that they can change their attitude through how they use their body. Nerve impulses flow both ways. She recommended they take five minutes a day and practice looking confident. If they do it enough, confidence will come. It's called, faking it until you make it.

She recommended to her class that they notice that positive emotions make their body expand, i.e., shoulders back, head held high. This is done without any conscious thought on their part.

On the other hand, negative emotions make their body shrink within itself. Shoulders droop, head goes down. It's almost as if they are trying to make themselves smaller; whereas, positive emotions make their bodies want to expand—shoulders up, head held high.

Abby stressed to the class that they always remember, "There is a pause between Stimulus and Response." That means that if someone is unkind to you, there is a second before you respond. You choose your response.

She asked the class if she were to kick any three people in the class, would they all react in the same way? Obviously, they would not! Each person chooses his own response. One may kick back; one may cry; one may look shocked.

EXERCISE: Going back to the chapter on body language, make a game out of asking kids to assume different body positions to simulate an emotion. Ask them how they feel in each emotion. The point is the posture they assume is the posture they will feel.

For example, Abby had her class stand up, raise their arms to the sky, look upward, and smile. In that position, she would ask them to feel sad. They could not. The lesson learned is that your body communicates to others how you feel and also communicates the same to you.

Abby saw the late Wayne Dyer when he was on stage in New York. He had a volunteer come up on stage, spoke to him, then asked him to put his arm straight out to the side at shoulder height. He then asked the person to think of the most pleasant thought he could imagine. Then Wayne tried to push his arm down, and he couldn't make it budge.

He then asked the man to put his arm in the same position, think of a really negative, sad thought, and Wayne pushed his arm down to his side quickly and easily. The point Wayne Dyer was making is our thoughts not only reflect our attitudes but also our bodies which reflect our attitude.

Abby recalls the story she heard told about three men building a cathedral. A passerby asked the first man what he was doing, and the man replied, "Digging a hole." The second man replied, "I'm making a wall." The third man happily responded, "I'm building a cathedral." This is a perfect example of attitude. Each man was doing the same job but saw their jobs differently. It is always a choice of how people see things.

After her experiences and her research, Abby decided to make attitude training a major portion of her training for her own kids and any class she taught outside the home. It applied to everyone, every age, every walk of life.

Attitude is a mindset—how an individual sees a situation. For example, the most common question asked when looking at a glass of water filled halfway is, "What do you see?" Do you see the glass half-full or half-empty?"

Abby focused on how someone can change from having a negative attitude to having a positive attitude. Her conclusion always starts with Step Number One: **AWARENESS!**

The average person has between 50,000 and 60,000 thoughts a day as determined by scientific research. No one is aware of the constant barrage of thoughts, but they can do one thing— TAKE CONTROL by becoming aware of the thoughts. As they do, thoughts then become self-talk. This awareness is where each individual can take control.

Have a MANTRA ready to repeat which will counteract the negative thought. Remember the three-year old boy who repeated his mantra on the way to school. Adopt his three phrases; "I am smart!" "I am blessed!" "I can do anything!"

Abby had her classes write down three phrases related to what they wanted to be or have. She had them write all three on one card and make two or three copies—one for their wallets, one for their mirrors, and one to keep with them in order to counteract any negative thought that came to their minds.

The second thing Abby was able to teach them was what she covered in the body language section. How you stand relates to how you feel. How you look reveals how you feel. She stresses to all of her classes that this is where choice comes in. If you choose to feel good, make yourself look good by your posture and facial expression, and control your thoughts. She emphasized that these recommendations take time and practice but are well worth the effort.

Abby acknowledged how stressful the jobs in the transportation department are. She asked them to start a daily routine beginning with looking at themselves in the mirror and telling themselves a compliment, i.e., "I have a great sense of humor!" "I am a special person." "I really care for people!"

She stressed to her classes that building a positive attitude as a habit feels good, and it lasts as long as they remain aware. She encouraged class members to keep a list of things they were proud of, people they loved, activities they loved.

In every class, Abby asked each participant to write down the name of someone they view as having a good attitude and write why they think that.

Second, she asked each person to describe someone they know who has a bad attitude and why they think that.

Without naming names, each class member could describe the differences between a person with a good or a bad attitude.

In their handouts, Abby included a very simple process on how to change attitude.

DAILY PROCESS: (Establish as a HABIT—it feels good!)

- **A.M. - Wake up: repeat to yourself (or aloud) your personal mantra, i.e. I am special," "I love my job," "I am heathy, fit, and happy," whatever feels good to you and whatever it is you desire. (Ignore that little voice in your head that is not "buying in." Eventually, it will!)**

- **DURING THE DAY: Make the following a conditioned response whenever you become aware of a negative thought:**
  - **Place three fingers lightly on your heart (or chest area)**
  - **Inhale deeply**
  - **Visualize what you most desire (realistically)**
  - **Exhale**
  - **Relax**
  - **Feel**
  - **Repeat until you get the feeling you desire**

- **P.M. - Head on your pillow: choose to say, see, and feel your three intentions or desires. Allow only the thoughts you want in your head. It feels good!**

Abby emphasized to her transportation students the same thing she emphasizes to her own children. **THE ENTIRE POINT IS** everyone can control their attitude through posture, facial expression and thoughts. It doesn't matter what happens to us in life. What matters is how we react to what happens to us. We have that power because we are the writers, directors and producers of our lives.

Why is it important to control our attitudes? It affects people's perception of us, and most importantly, it affects how we feel.

THE KEYS TO MASTERY OF ATTITUDE:

- **AWARENESS OF SELF-TALK (thoughts recognized by you) AND**
- **AWARENESS OF BODY LANGUAGE**

The thing that I learned as a diplomat is that human relations ultimately make a huge difference.

- Madeline Albright

Look for positives in everyone!!

CHAPTER THIRTEEN

PEOPLE SKILLS

A great way to remember a list, a group of items, names, dates, principles or even points of a talk is to "stack" them as you did in Chapter Eight, The Baker's Dozen. Our minds can remember pictures more readily than it can remember words. If Abby is giving a talk, she will have her points "stacked" one on top of another in her head, so that if her mind goes blank, she can refer to the picture in her mind.

The amazing part of "stacking" is that you will be able to teach this stack to your child or student in five minutes–because you will be using pictures.

After reading about **S-A-V-E** and the **Code of Ethics**, Abby has one more group of principles, a stack of nine human relation skills. In order to remember them, clearly picture the following mental pictures in your head–the clearer the picture you can see, the better you will be able to remember it. The underlined words are the ones you want to "see." Don't think about it, just see it.

HUMAN RELATIONS STACK

In your mind's eye, picture an <u>ice statue</u> of a <u>cheerleader</u> with <u>headphones</u> on. Look closely and you'll see, as in a cartoon, <u>bubbles</u> coming out of her head, indicating she is thinking. What she is thinking about is a <u>thermostat</u>, so she won't melt. In her <u>praying hands</u> is a huge <u>candy bar</u>. On the wrapper of the candy bar is a big <u>C</u> and a <u>plus sign</u> (<u>+</u>).

Repeat this until every student as the picture in their minds and can repeat the picture backwards.

Each mental picture represents a human relations principle. They are as follows:

MENTAL PICTURE   PRINCIPLE

Ice Statue: Accept people as they are.

Cheerleader: Be enthusiastic in all you do.

Headphones: Listen. It is the greatest compliment you can pay someone.

Bubbles: Thoughts. Your thoughts create your world.

Thermostat: You cannot control what happens to you, but you can always control your reactions.

Praying hands: Accept what is, e.g., Serenity Prayer.

Candy bar: Treat others as you wish to be treated.

C: Do not criticize other people. No one ever appreciates being criticized. Could you go through an entire day without once complaining? Without once criticizing? Wouldn't it be great if everybody in the world could do that? In one class, there were three girls who shared an apartment, each with her own room. If somebody complained, they got a C, criticize, condemn or complain tacked onto their door. None of the girls wanted a C placed on their door for having done that.

+ sign: Look for the positives in everyone.

The key to successfully implementing these principles is to make sure each is used with sincerity. You can use these principles to manipulate people, but then they're not human relation principles; they're merely tools of manipulation. Sincerity is what makes them human relation principles.

REMEMBER the old adage, "If you always do what you've always done, you'll always get what you've always got." If you can incorporate these basic human relation principles into your life, you will definitely find that your relationships will improve.

LONG-RANGE ASSIGNMENT

* Choose one of the principles in the stack and use it for at least two weeks to improve your relationship with someone you see on a regular basis.
* Complete the following chart and keep it as a reminder of your commitment to the principle.

TIPS COMMITMENT SHEET

(Choose one of the principles in the stack to apply to the person of your choice.)

TIP CHOSEN:

WHY DID YOU CHOOSE THIS TIP?

PERSON WITH WHOM YOU EXPECT TO USE TIP:

ON WHAT SITUATION DO YOU THINK YOU CAN USE THIS TIP?

WHAT DO YOU HOPE WILL HAPPEN?

WHAT WILL YOU DO IF THE TIP DOES NOT WORK THE FIRST TIME?

HOW MANY TIMES WILL YOU ATTEMPT TO USE THIS TIP?

RESULT: WRITE A DETAILED PARAGRAPH ABOUT THE RESULTS OF THIS COMMITMENT AFTER USING IT FOR TWO WEEKS.

"The view you
adopt for yourself
profoundly affects
the way you lead
your life."

- Carol Dweck, PhD, <u>Mindset</u>

CHAPTER FOURTEEN

TOLERATIONS

Tolerations are what you put up with in life–environmental issues, stress, restrictions, messy rooms—things that are part of your life but do not add to the quality of your life. Tolerations could include people, situations, behaviors – yours or others–your environment, your body, your feelings, your problems, pressures, family members, clutter, traffic, computer, neighbors, pets, restrictions, stress, inadequacies, events, friends, your job, your situation in life.

Recognizing the tolerations of kids is the beginning of the elimination, where possible, of those things in life that impede their progress.

Abby stresses that in order to change, you have to identify what are you putting up with. As long as you have tolerations, you won't have peace of mind; you will have stress. If your goal is to be the best that you can be in every way, start being aware of and listing every toleration in your life.

Step one is always awareness. Once you are aware of a toleration, then you have an opportunity to make a plan. Once the thing, person or situation is brought to the forefront of your mind, you'll be better prepared to deal with it. For example, if someone's always harping on you and you tolerate it, you're under stress. You have two choices: leave the vicinity of the person or disconnect, mentally check-out when that person is on your back.

A toleration could involve a family member, someone you love. Abby uses the example of her mother whom she loved dearly. After Abby moved to another state, she would talk to her every

Sunday night, and every Sunday night she would end up annoyed because her mom was still talking to her as if she were a small child. Finally, Abby learned to disconnect. She could hear her mom's words, but she didn't react emotionally. That took time; it takes a lot of effort, but Abby recommends that if you are being upset unjustly, just disconnect. The person probably believes their advice is for your own good, and you know they care; but those words are still a source of stress.

You cannot control what happens to you, but you can always control how you react. Do not allow anybody to push your buttons. This is a lesson that you can pass on to your child, emphasizing that he or she may not be able to control what happens to them, but they can always control how they react. Their reaction should always be in keeping with how they want to be treated; namely, with respect.

One way to address tolerations with children or students is to have them keep a record of what they are tolerating on a daily basis.

WHAT AM I TOLERATING?   HOW I PLAN TO HANDLE IT:

By recognizing what someone is "tolerating" on a regular basis is the first step in alleviating the negative affects on yourself or your child. Again, awareness is always step one in order to change. You cannot change that with which you are unaware.

Abby hopes that the mastery of the two acronyms (S-A-V-E and C-L-A-P) can enable every parent to joyfully and successfully raise a CONFIDENT, happy child.

PART THREE

BULLYING AND MENTORING

BULLYING IS A NATIONAL EPIDEMIC

- Macklemore

CHAPTER FIFTEEN

BULLYING CAN DESTROY A CHILD'S CONFIDENCE

Before Abby gets into the specifics as to what a parent or a teacher can do, she wants you to be aware of the actual definition of the word "bullying" and take a look into some of the reasons why kids bully.

> **"Bullying" is defined as negative aggressive behavior that is repeated and is intentional by someone who thinks he/she has more power (older, bigger) with the intent to gain power over another person.**

Almost everyone has been picked on by somebody else at some time in their lives. Yes, Abby believes we all have been bullied to some degree, and that is what we want to discuss— "degree," meaning "being picked on vs. being bullied." **"Intent" may be the only difference between teasing and bullying**, and that can be a very fine line separating them.

Is a child being bullied because of race, religion, ethnic background, appearance, family's background? These grounds are all totally unacceptable. In order to raise a confident child, the existence of bullying has to be addressed.

As a parent or teacher, you have to be aware of the various types of bullying, which <u>usually</u> fall into one of the following categories:

- **Exclusion** (Most common) - gossiping, rumors, rejection, excluding from the group.

- **Put downs** (Second most common) - teasing, name calling.
- **Intimidation** (Scared but not physically or verbally assaulted) - taking possessions, taunting, extortion, more serious threats, dirty looks, threats.
- **Unwanted physical contact** (most obvious) - pushing, shoving, kicking, defacing property.

Abby asks, "Is your child or student experiencing one or more of these types of bullying?"

How do teasing and bullying differ? Teasing is POSITIVE. It shows that you are liked/accepted. It is playful, a pat on the back. Bullying is HURTFUL; it shows that you are not liked or accepted.

What do you tell a child to do when they are bullied or witness bullying? When Abby worked with elementary students, she encouraged them to react to bullying whenever they witness it with the slogan used in New York advertising: **SEE SOMETHING - SAY SOMETHING.**

She also learned that children as young as first grade were aware that **"snitches get stitches."** Abby had never heard that term until she started doing her Bully-Be-Gone program in tough inner-city schools.

Obviously, no parent wants his child to be bullied; no teacher wants bullies in her class. Physically and/or verbally hurting someone impedes that child's development not only in school but also in life.

Abby points out that people need air to breathe, food to nourish their bodies, acceptance and validation to nourish their souls. Everybody wants to be liked. A child who is bullied knows he is not liked. If he knows he is not liked, why bother........? And here is where the ultimate fear of a parent comes in—suicide.

There are two types of hurts: the <u>outside</u>–a cut, a bruise, a scrape on the knee–those heal, and **the <u>inside</u>**–taunts, name-calling, exclusion–they scar. That's what bullying does; it leaves scars.

At the beginning of Abby's anti-bullying program for kids, she highlights the significance of bullying by having students respond to the following True or False questions:

TRUE OR FALSE:
1. **Thousands of children stay home from school every day because they fear what is going to happen to them at school or going to and from school.**
   (**TRUE:** National Association of School Psychologists)

FACT:
* Most bullying occurs on playground or crowded hallways.
* Each day 160,000 students miss school for fear of being bullied.
* 1 out of 5 students in a school bullying statistics and cyber bullying statistics study admit to being a bully, or doing some "bullying."

2. **Bullying is more of a problem in high school than middle school.**
   (**FALSE**: The frequency was higher among 6-8th grade students than among high school students. "Bullying Behaviors Among US Youth," Journal of the American Medical Association.)

FACTS:
* Only approximately one-third of the student population are bullies. The rest are ByStanders.
* Statistics show that third graders will report bullying to a teacher 36% of the time; by sixth grade the reporting of bullying incidences goes down to 3%.
* Aggression starts at early age–nursery schools; 2 years old.
* Bullying causes misery to others - sometimes for a lifetime.

- Most hurt is the bully himself/herself - 60% end up in jail.
- Bullies frequently turn into antisocial adults—wife beaters/child abusers.

3. **It is not bullying if the Target and Aggressor are friends.** (**FALSE**: Bullying is when a person feels afraid of what will happen—physical or emotional. This can occur among friends.)

FACTS:
- Bullying can be a desperate, damaging way to socialize, to feel included.
- Bullies are different: they think others are hostile.

4. **Almost half of middle- and high-school students avoid using school bathrooms for fear of being harassed or assaulted.** (**TRUE**: Anna Mulrine, "Once Bullied, Now Bullies—With Guns," U.S. News & World Report)

FACT:
- School bullying statistics reveal that 43% fear harassment in the bathroom at school.

5. **Bullies are never targets.** (**FALSE**: About one third of bullies are themselves targets of bullying, and these children have a higher risk of depression and suicidal thoughts than other children: R. Kaltiala-Heino et al., "Bullying, Depression and Suicidal Ideation in Finnish Adolescents: School Survey," British Medical Journal 319 (1999): 349-351)

FACTS:
- Earlier Bullies (Pre 1970's) were generally portrayed as unlikable, generally unpopular individuals who were public nuisances. One example is Reggie from "Archie Comics" which was created in 1942. Reggie is immature, self-centered, egotistical, and enjoys playing pranks at the expense of others.

- They were often put in their place by kinder, more popular, and more respected individuals.
- Starting around 1970, depiction of bullies tended to take on the form of attractive individuals who were popular and tended to pick on nerdy type characters.

6. **Children who are picked on over and over are more likely to be depressed, feel bad about themselves, and stop doing things with others. Some may even end up killing themselves.**
   (**TRUE**)

FACTS: Watch for the warning signs:
- The child is afraid to walk to or from school
- The child does not want to ride the school bus
- The child comes home with clothing or personal items damaged
- The child seems socially isolated with few, if any, friends
- The child appears sad or depressed about going to school
- The child appears to be sleeping more than usual or appears tired as if they have not gotten enough sleep

TARGETS OF BULLYING, OR VICTIMS, MAY BE "DIFFERENT,"
Frequently they have one or more of the following characteristics. They may
- be more sensitive, cautious, and quieter than other kids
- be more anxious or nervous or fearful
- withdraw from confrontation of any kind and cry when attacked
- not do well in gym or reading in front of the class
- become submissive when picked on, don't fight back–easy target
- be fearful their physical weakness may make them vulnerable.
- be smaller in stature, overweight, skinny, has red hair, wears old tattered clothes
- have low self-esteem
- exhibit submissiveness

- appear depressed or sad
- have a limited sense of humor

There are many famous people who were bullied as children: Lady Gaga, Sandra Bullock, Rihanna, Justin Timberlake, Tyra Banks, Kate Winslet, Kate Middleton, Jennifer Lawrence, Christian Bale, Jackie Chan, Jessica Alba, Taylor Swift, Mila Kunas, Chris Rock, Miley Cyrus, Tom Cruise, Madonna, Barack Obama, Christina Aguilera, Steven Spielberg, Kristen Stewart, Bill Clinton, Victoria Beckham, Tiger Woods, Prince Harry, Daniel Radcliffe, and many more.

Why were these people bullied? Because they were different in some way: hair color, size—small, overweight, skinny—shy, quiet, racially or ethnically different, wrong crowd, wrong clothes, wrong home location, and so much more. Bottom line: they were different in some way.

Obviously, no one likes a bully, but frequently kids will turn against a victim also—to stay on the right side of the bully. While bullying hurts, it is the social isolation that is most damaging to victims. This isolation leads to loneliness and/ or dislike of school.

Abby's objective in working with students is to train bystanders to take an active part in any bullying situation they witness, as long as no weapons are in existence.

She encourages bystanders to help by remember the acronym S-A-F-E

S - SAFETY is first concern for everyone involved
A - Get ADULT quickly
F - FACE up to the bully
E - EMPOWER target by siding with and helping where possible

When Abby asked students why more bystanders don't intervene, their responses include:

- They think, "It's none of my business."
- They fear getting hurt or becoming another victim.
- They feel powerless to stop the bully.
- They don't like the victim or believe the victim "deserves" it.
- They don't want to draw attention to themselves.
- They fear retribution.
- They think that telling adults won't help or it may make things worse.
- They don't know what to do.

Those who have seen TV show, "What Would You Do?" can readily relate to bullying situations. They can view the incidents safely from their homes and see how important it is for bystanders to become involved.

Students have also indicated that bystanders who don't intervene or don't report the bullying often suffer negative consequences themselves, because they may experience:

- Pressure to participate in the bullying.
- Afraid to speak to anyone about the bullying.
- Powerlessness to stop bullying.
- Vulnerability to becoming victimized.
- Fear of associating with the victim, the bully, or the bully's pals.
- Guilt for not having defended the victim.

(She encourages adults to think about what bothers you. What are you self-conscious about? **Are any of these your buttons?** hair color, size, cries easily, too good or not good at schoolwork, racial/ethnic taunting, right crowd, right clothes, family, weight, worries a lot.)

When someone has pushed one of your child's or student's buttons, Abby encourages them to try one or a combination of the following:

a. Ignore the bully
b. Try to diffuse with humor
c. Speak up to defend yourself
d. If possible, leave the area immediately before anything physical occurs

She **also encourages kids to plan for the next time** this same person tries to get to you. In all likelihood, there will be a next time. People who like to push the buttons of others usually try again and the second and third time it might be worse. When it happens, **remind your child that**

- It is most important to be safe.
- Winning is not who is best at put-downs.
- Winning is taking care of your own emotions.

One way a parent or teacher can help a child who has been bullied is to work with them to APPEAR ASSERTIVE. She suggests that they practice LOOKING ASSERTIVE.

EXERCISE: In the following exercise, Abby recommends you rate the youngster on a score of 1 to 5, 1 is appearing weak; 5 is appearing strong. A simple exercise that can be practiced around the kitchen table or in a classroom is to ask class (or family members) to stand up–FREEZE!! Choose one person to be the monitor. Ask the monitor, "Who looks assertive?" Ask why that choice was made. The reasons given will be enlightening to everyone.

Does it matter if the person actually is assertive? NO! It matters how they appear to others, especially the bully. Abby recommends families to make this a fun activity with a serious purpose.

When asked, "How do you look assertive?" Abby relied, "It's simple. Merely stand tall with your shoulders back, your head up high. Put a slight scow or a look of confidence on your face rather than a look of fear. Avoid the "deer in the headlights" look. Pretend you're playing a role in a play, and you are the tough guy. Practice your "look" in a mirror and decide which "face" you prefer.

She pointed out that the New York City police train ladies to **NOT** look like victims when walking on the street. Will a potential bully or robber pick on someone who walks with their shoulders back, head held high and a no-nonsense look on their face or the person with shoulders stooped, eyes down, and a scared look on their face? They will probably choose the latter. There are plenty of other potential victims nearby.

The goal is to LOOK ASSERTIVE AND CONFIDENT!

BULLY MAGNETS have their
- Head down
- Shoulders slumped
- Face scared
- Eyes down
- Voice weak

A more ASSERTIVE/CONFIDENT person
- Observes everything but avoids eye contact
- Has shoulders back
- Head up
- Speaks with strength
- Engages others

Abby also encourages the victims of bullying to protect themselves by using the elements of the acronym, G-I-F-T. Remember, protecting yourself is a G-I-F-T.

1. **GET away as quickly as possible.**
2. **IGNORE initial push or hit, if possible.**

Gail A. Cassidy

3. **FACE** up to the bully.
4. **TELL** adult.

Abby reminds the victim to remember that they are giving control to the other person if they respond by whimpering or crying. Not reacting means that the victim wins and the bully loses because the victim stayed in control. If a bully cannot intimidate the victim, the bully feels threatened. He/she realizes he is not scaring anyone, therefore, quickly understands that his bullying position is weakened.

The two acronyms to remember are S-A-F-E (S - SAFETY is first concern for everyone involved; **A - Get ADULT quickly; F - FACE up to the bully; E - EMPOWER target by siding with and helping where possible) for the bystander and G-I-F-T (1. GET away as quickly as possible; IGNORE the initial push or hit, if possible; 3. FACE up to the bully; TELL an adult) for the victim.**

EXERCISE: Ask your child or student to write about one incident of bullying that they saw happen or heard about. When Abby brought this program to inner-city elementary schools, she would always ask if anyone here is a bully, and invariably a couple of smiling little third grade boys would pop their hands up. At that point they were not really aware of bullying. At the end of the program they did recognize the seriousness of the subject. Having kids write or tell their stories is a great jumping-off point for discussion.

142

"The time to be happy is now; the place to be happy is here; and the way to be happy is by helping others."

- Charles Engelhardt

CHAPTER SIXTEEN

TEENAGERS AND PARENTS AS MENTORS

That you have chosen to read this book, Abby believes speaks volumes about you, the loudest being your desire to raise a confident, happy child.

In this chapter, Abby wants to address the problem of kids who may be having some challenges with some aspect of school — whether it be friends or teachers, classes, fear, anxiety – whatever it is that's making school a less-than-positive experience for them.

Choosing to read this book is a clear indication that you are interested in not only raising a confident child but also creating a bully-free culture, including the forbidding of racism in any form.

You may feel that you have been so fortunate so far in life that you want to make sure your children have that same opportunity, or maybe you have experienced challenges at some time that you want to prevent others from experiencing. You just may desire the good feeling that comes with making a difference in the lives of others. Whatever reason you're reading to learn about helping create a safe, bully-free culture, Abby applauds your decision.

Helping others not only feels good, it changes lives. Philosopher, Albert Schweitzer, said, "Every person I have known who has been truly happy has learned to serve others."

Abby's primary objective is to explain to you exactly what creating a bully-free culture means and why it is so important not only for the person–child or student–but also for the knowledge and understanding that you will come away with.

Actor, Denzel Washington, believes that his success in life is due to a mentor (someone who cared about him and validated him) he had as a teenager in an after-school boys' club. He was born and raised in Mount Vernon, New York, a rowdy neighborhood—the streets were tough and gangs were prevalent. He lived in a bad section; and had he taken the wrong path, he certainly would not be the famous Denzel Washington we know, the actor who has done such a great job in the movies.

A couple of years ago, Abby read Denzel's book, *A Hand to Guide Me*. In it, he showcases how mentors—including parents and teachers—shape the lives of people we all know and respect, from baseball legend Hank Aaron, Mohammed Ali, Bob Woodward (the reporter during the Nixon era). You have probably heard of Yogi Berra, Danny Glover, the actor, Whoopi Goldberg, and many other names of the over 60 famous people he interviewed. Every one of them had a mentor, somebody who believed in them and encouraged them.

Washington writes about how the famous people he interviewed for his book—actors, athletes, musicians, doctors, lawyers, politicians, business leaders—all had the guidance of someone or something, at some time or other. They all built on that guidance, internalized it and made it their own. He believes that if you have achieved any kind of real and lasting success, if you've made any kind of difference, it's more than likely there was someone there to help point the way.

According to Abby, most of us have had a mentor at some point in our lives. He or she may have come in the form of a teacher, a parent, a relative, an aunt, uncle, maybe a guardian, an older friend, a counselor, a coach, a minister, priest, rabbi, cleric, tutor, expert – somebody who believed in you, encouraged you to be the best you can be, and someone who had a positive influence on you. She wants you to think about the people in your life. Who has made a difference? Who do you know who believes in you?

In some instances, parents are the best choice for playing the role of mentor to their child, and sometimes someone a step outside of the immediate family may be the person best suited to work with your child, like an aunt, close friend, religious leader, etc. The mentor's job is to use the principles of S-A-V-E to help the child to do the best he/she possibly can, e.g., help maximize the child's potential. Stepping out of the role of parent or teacher and adopting the role of mentor may make the process easier to adopt. Abby believes that parents are sensitive to the needs of their child and know if they are too close or too un-objective to be an effective mentor.

It's amazing how having somebody believe in you really makes you want to do the best that you can do. Sometimes people around us, our parents or people who are close to us, are just too busy surviving, earning a living, and that's where you, the reader, come in; and that is exactly what you want for your child, someone to accept and encourage our child to be the best that he or she can be. Having a mentor for your child is having an opportunity to impact your child's life in a positive manner. Think about who it is in your life who encouraged you. Keep thinking about that as you decide who is best to work with your child.

To refresh your memory, Abby suggests you write down the people in your life who have mentored you, believed in you, encouraged you. Keep those people in mind. She knows who they are in her life. One was her church minister who convinced his church Board to pay one quarter of her tuition for college because her parents would have bought her a new Chevrolet convertible, but they would not pay a dime toward her schooling. They thought she was "too big for her britches." They believed that "nice Irish girls stayed home." Abby's aunt was her mentor. She came to her house every night for weeks to help Abby master one course that she found very difficult; and once she "got it," it was easy– smooth sailing thereafter. It was Abby's Aunt Nancy who hired her for a

Gail A. Cassidy

summer job working at her insurance company. She believed in Abby. Those two people had a tremendous impact on Abby's life.

EXERCISE: LIST THREE PEOPLE YOU CONSIDER MENTORS IN YOUR LIFE.

MAKE ANOTHER LIST OF FIVE PEOPLE YOU ADMIRE, DEAD OR ALIVE.
After each person's name, write WHY you admire them.

1.
2.
3.
4.
5.

THE "WHY" is most significant. For example, Abby admires Michael Jordon, even though she does not follow basketball. She admires how he handled his fame. Another person on her list is Oprah Winfrey for the impact she has had on people. Another is Hillary Clinton because she was driven by her desire to help women and children long before she had ever met her husband. Another is Benjamin Franklin because of his brilliance and humor.

Again, it is the "why" you admire someone that is significant. The "why" reveals what is important to you in general.

PART FOUR

TEENAGERS AND MENTORS

"A mentor is someonewho allows you to see the hope inside yourself."

- Oprah Winfrey

CHAPTER SEVENTEEN

THE IMPORTANCE OF A MENTOR

Keep in mind that a mentor is a confidant, someone who listens without judgment and helps a child make their best decisions. Why is mentoring important? Take a look at the facts.

Statistically, we lose up to 50 percent of our high school graduates before graduation. When Abby says 50 percent, she is including those who graduate, but graduate as functional illiterates. They might know the words "and," "the," "dog," "cat," but they can't understand the meaning of a paragraph. They can't read a bus schedule. They can't figure out their bills; they can't figure out any legal forms—insurance, divorce papers, deeds, etc. They're functionally illiterate.

In the United States, we have a high number of dropouts, maybe not in your school or the schools around you, but drop-out rates are high in some of the inner-city schools where English is a second language. There are many students who cannot speak English. After a hurricane devastated their country, numerous Haitians arrived in the U.S. who don't speak the language. Hopefully, they will be able to be trained well enough to qualify for graduation.

During a Back to School Night, Abby met with the parents of her Haitian student, a girl who had no accent at all even though she had been in the country less than a year. Her parents, on the other hand, were very difficult to understand. Their accents were very thick. The next day in class, Abby asked the daughter how she shed her accent so quickly. She said she worked with a tape recorder every day, practicing the English she heard on

TV. She was determined to fit in, to not be different from her classmates. The point in, "where there is a will, there is a way. This girl proved that adage to be true. Her parents were her mentors. They encouraged her to succeed in a country foreign to them all.

As a nation, Abby believes we have a major problem with those who fail to graduate. What happens to those kids? A large percentage end up in jail. She found that we have 2.2 million people in jails at an estimated $50,000 a year – that's what it costs each year to keep an inmate imprisoned. There is a 66 per cent recidivism rate. That means 66 percent of those who leave jail end up back in jail. Wow, that's two-thirds of all prison releases return within three years. Forty-four billion dollars are spent annually on prisons alone. To repeat, a high percentage of dropouts end up in prison. They drop out because they believe it is better for them outside of school.

Abby worries that if a student is coming to school and hating it, is being bullied, is being mistreated and is failing, why would they want to stay in school? It's safer outside for them. In their minds, it is safer belonging to a gang. Obviously, gang affiliation is not safe in the long run.

She believes that the principles of mentoring can save eight out of ten potential dropouts from going to prison. That would be a savings of millions of dollars a year. Overall, the total number of people behind bars, again, is 2.2 million people. This is one reason why she wants a mentoring program where kids feel safe and are less likely to be bullied. She wants a program where people feel safe, feel accepted, and feel validated.

After the Kids Mentoring Kids program began in one of the schools, a mother called and said that because of the bullying her son experienced daily, she couldn't even get him to go to school. Once he started working with a mentor, he changed dramatically.

Because he knew a junior in high school, he felt important, and he felt protected. He believed he was safe just because he knew and was accepted by an upperclassman.

The Boys' and Girls' Club of America, who have adult mentors working with students, did a study to determine the effectiveness of their mentoring. Their results indicated the following:

- 46 percent of students who are mentored are less likely to begin using illegal drugs,
- 27 percent are less likely to start using alcohol;
- 37 percent decrease in lying to parents – I don't know how they measure that, but that's the statistic they presented;
- 52 percent are less likely to skip school;
- 33 percent less likely to get into fights; and
- 55 percent had a better attitude toward school.

These statistics are encouraging; however, their situation is different from Kids Mentoring Kids. The Boys' and Girls' Club of America have adults as their mentors. They therefore have the disadvantage of having to find unrelated adults as mentors which takes, on average, six months to line up a mentor with a mentee. The reason it takes so long to match mentor with a mentee is that adults working with kids other than their own have to be fingerprinted and background checked. The process does take a long time.

The good news is that 58 percent of the mentored children improved their schoolwork and 65 percent had much higher levels of self-confidence, and that is as a result of someone taking the time to listen, to accept, validate, ultimately, making a difference.

Abby encourages you to think of a mentor as a coach with their role being to encourage, to guide, to accept. Kids have to know that everything they tell you, about himself or her family is confidential. From a mentor's perspective, the only difference would be if you see that there's physical, sexual or emotional abuse. That has to be reported to the authorities in your school or to the police, according to your school policy. Serious situations like these have to be taken care of immediately.

If you are a mentor and feel that there is a possibility of an attempted suicide, you know the situation has to be reported according to your school's policy, as does knowledge about illegal weapons, substance abuse – alcohol, liquor – alcohol, liquor or drugs, or if you feel a child is a danger to himself or others. Other than those legal, policy-related exceptions, everything a child tells a mentor is confidential.

Many years ago Abby took a seminar on child-rearing, and the instructor asked the class how they would react if their fifteen year-old daughter came home from a date and told them she had made love in the back seat of a car. The class reacted strongly, "I'd ground her." "I'd take away her privileges." "I'd have a long, serious talk with her, etc." After numerous participants voiced their indignation, the lecturer quietly said, "And you have taught her never to tell you anything again."

Not long thereafter, Abby's daughter came home and told her she had been at a party where the kids trashed the basement, describing in detail how they put broom handles through the ceiling tiles and totally wrecked the place. With great restraint Abby didn't respond. She let her talk. Her daughter ended up saying in disgust that she would never hang around with those kids again. Had Abby jumped in with her pontifications and lots of pre-determined judgment, her daughter may have defended her friends.

The point is – listen completely; don't judge; then rationally discuss.

A mentor —teacher, aunt, minister, friend, parent—is a coach who is encouraging, guiding and accepting. A mentor will look to see the talent, the ability, the specialness in your child, even more so than the child sees in himself or herself. A mentor helps bring out these special traits and characteristics.

Mentors are coaches; they are not therapists. Therapists go back into people's lives and try to figure out what made them the way they are. A mentor's job is to accept the child as they are and allow them to recognize what is special about themselves. A mentor is someone who has a positive impact on the life of another person, someone who recognizes and brings out more talent, ability and specialness within their mentee than the mentee sees in himself.

Abby's overall goals are not only numerous, but they are also huge and have long-range significance. She wants to prevent kids

- from dropping out of school,
- from being bullied,
- from participating in gangs,
- from engaging in teen violence and its ramifications, and
- to give them the opportunity to maximize their potential,
- To have inner confidence.

She recognizes that parents and teachers are major influences on children, and the kids need their help. What she desires is to have kids work up to their ability, to have teachers experience greater satisfaction, and for parents to be proud of their kids. Teachers love to see their kids doing well. Administrators love to have excellent schools. Parents love to have happy kids. These positive outcomes can come to fruition with your help.

EXERCISE: WHAT ARE YOUR GREATEST FEARS FOR YOUR CHILD OR YOUR STUDENT.

WHY DO YOU HAVE THOSE FEARS?

WHAT CAN YOU DO TO ELIMINATE THOSE FEARS?

WHO WOULD BE A GOOD MENTOR FOR YOUR CHILD?

As a parent, can you adopt this role? The next chapter provides more detailed information on mentoring.

"Seek First to Understand; Then to Be Understood."

- Stephen Covey

CHAPTER EIGHTEEN

MENTORING POINTERS

Now you know the "why" of mentoring–why it is so vitally important to help children to gain confidence and self-respect. Abby hopes she has made it clear that once a child owns those qualities, they'll be able to do well on their own.

How do we get kids to believe in themselves? How can a mentor prepare them to be citizens of the world? How can you get them to see the value within themselves? What can you do to motivate them to learn? How can you provide hope and opportunity?

Who are the people in your life who have mentored you, believed in you, encouraged you? Keep them in mind. Abby knows who they are in her life. She has already mentioned her church minister and her aunt. Who are yours?

She cautions you to be aware of the beliefs you have about yourself, your background, your abilities, your future. Even George W. Bush talks about the importance of belief. "America is a Nation with a mission - and that mission comes from our most basic beliefs." As America is shaped by beliefs, so are our individual lives. Abby is assuming you believe in the importance of what you and/or a mentor can do to help your child or your student.

Whether a mentor is working with their own child or with a student, they will find that having something in writing will help, something that will allow the child to determine where and how he wants to proceed. The Mentoring Preparation Form entails no pressure, no grammar checks; this is for the child's benefit to write what they've accomplished since their last session. If they've accomplished nothing, that's just a "what is," it's not a judgment. If a mentor is working with students, they are going to work with kids who may have backgrounds different from theirs. No one knows what's going on their homes or what is preventing them from succeeding.

Abby worked with a student who at one time had been a great student. Suddenly she stopped working, and she had a bad attitude. She was always tired. Abby didn't know why. One day she called her into her classroom after class and asked if there were a problem? She said, "Yes, my mother is in the hospital, I have to go in every night with my little sisters, take care of them, do my homework, take care of my mother." Her mother was terminally ill. There was a legitimate reason why she was not performing as she had been.

Some kids who are being mentored may not want to share the problems they're facing now. If they have obvious challenges, their mentor should ask them if they would write what's bothering them. Once they have identified their problem(s), have them write what they see as the opportunities that are available to them – meaning is there a teacher who will work with them on their math or their English or their science or their spelling, or whatever it is?

A mentor isn't responsible for improving their grades. He or she may not be good in math, so will not to be the one that helps, but could possibly direct them to someone who could.

The mentored child is also going to write what they want to complete with their mentor during this time. Initially, they might be reluctant to actively participant, but as they start talking, the mentor has to listen carefully to what they are saying and how they are saying it, then decide how to best help them. Finally, the mentor can ask them to write what they intend to do by the next meeting or phone call. The child's forms will eventually show a progression from what they initially stated as their problems to how they are handling their challenges.

MENTORING PREPARATION FORM

NAME: _____   Scheduled Session_____

What I have accomplished since our last session:

What I didn't get done, but intended to:

The challenges and problems I'm facing now:

Opportunities that are available to me right now:

I want to work with my mentor during this call on:

At end of session: What I intend to do by the next call:

Additional Notes:

Signature _____ Date _____

Because this form is completed by the child, the child makes the decisions regarding the path she wants to take, without the influence of her parent. This could be a first step in taking control of her own life.

The mentored child should be encouraged to set up goals. Encourage the child to make a commitment and to be accountable for their actions. Accountability is an invaluable asset to internalize, and what a great help it will be to the mentee throughout their lives.

Kids may also want to know the benefits of working with a mentor.

TOP 15 BENEFITS OF WORKING WITH A MENTOR

1. They are familiar with you, your background, your interests, and your goals.
2. They can help you uncover dreams and activities that made you feel special.
3. They can help you to follow through on your life's purpose.
4. They can help you find greater happiness in your life.
5. They can help you learn how to complete your past.
6. They can help you restore your energy.
7. They can help you get your needs met.
8. They can help you capitalize on your skills and abilities.
9. They can help you plan to earn a good living wage.
10. They can help you live by your value system.
11. They can help you eliminate things in your life that are not in your best interests.
12. They can help you maintain an upbeat, positive attitude.
13. They can help you handle difficult, challenging situations.
14. They can help you develop a stronger community.
15. They can help you be the best person you can be.

10 Goals to Reach in the Next 90 Days according to the age of the child being mentored. Choose topics appropriate to your child or student and age level.

Select goals you want to accomplish in the areas you desire. When you see the right goals for yourself, you should feel excited, a little nervous, ready and willing to go for it! INCLUDE BENEFITS ANTICIPATED.

ENVIRONMENT:

Start Date	Finish Date	S.M.A.R.T. GOAL: Specific, Measurable, Action planned, Results oriented, Time phased.
_____	_____	_____
_____	_____	_____

GROOMING

_____	_____	_____
_____	_____	_____

DESIRED AREA OF IMPROVEMENT (select a specific topic)

_____	_____	_____
_____	_____	_____

RELATIONSHIPS WITH FAMILY MEMBERS OR FRIENDS (Be specific)

_____	_____	_____
_____	_____	_____

LISTENING (Be specific)

_____	_____	_____
_____	_____	_____

Here is a suggested list of items a child can talk about to their mentor.

THINGS TO TALK ABOUT WITH A PARENT OR TEACHER MENTOR

HOW YOU ARE?
* How you are feeling about yourself - good stuff and bad stuff
* How you are looking at your life
* How you are feeling about others.

WHAT HAS HAPPENED SINCE OUR LAST MEETING?
* What has occurred to you since the last call
* Breakthroughs and insights
* Any new choices or decisions made
* Personal news

WHAT YOU ARE WORKING ON?
* Progress report on your goals, projects and activities
* What you've done that you are proud of
* What you are coming up against

HOW I CAN HELP?
* Where are you stuck
* What you are curious about
* A plan of action
* A strategy or advice

WHAT IS NEXT?
* What is the next goal or project to take on
* What do you want next for yourself

MORE THINGS TO TALK ABOUT:
* How they are you feeling about themselves, is that good or bad?
* How they are looking at their lives.
* How they are feeling about others.
* What has occurred since the last meeting?
* Any breakthroughs?
* Any insights?

- New choices?
- Decisions?
- Any personal news?
- What they have done that they are proud of.
- What resistance have they encountered?
- Who's giving them a hard time?
- Can I explain something?
- Can I provide more information?
- Do they need help developing a plan?
- May I offer a strategy or advice?
- What is their next goal or project?

You'll be amazed how easy it is to see other people's problems. You'll also be amazed that you know some good solutions. We're a lot wiser than we think.

If you can, encourage them to set goals, smart goals. S-M-A-R-T. "S" stands for "**s**pecific", e.g., I want to increase my English grade by 10 points. **"M"** It's measurable. **"A"** It's **a**ction planned. How are you going to do that? **"R"** **R**esults-oriented, e.g., I want to increase my English grade point by 10 points, by handing in all of my work on time and studying for my vocabulary quizzes; and, as a result, I'll be on the honor roll by **"T"** **(time-phased)** December 1st.

This goal is specific, it is measurable, it's action-planned, it's results oriented and it's time phased. Abby believes we should all set goals that are "SMART" goals.

CHALLENGE:
Give your child unconditional love and well-defined boundaries, mix it up with the 13 tips, S-A-V-E, and the Child's Creed, and you find yourself with a confident child!! Keep in mind, this isn't about you, the parent or the teacher; it's about providing the support your child needs to believe in himself, to possess that magic coin! (See Introduction for Magic Coin.)

For more information about mentoring, Abby has three books for your consideration:

- *The Validating Mentor* by Gail Cassidy
- *The Validating Mentor Workbook* by Gail Cassidy
- *Kids Mentoring Kids* by Gail Cassidy

All three books are found on amazon.com.

Everyone has his own specific vocation or mission in life. Therein he cannot be replaced, nor can his life be repeated. Thus, everyone's task is as unique as is his specific opportunity to implement it.

- Viktor Frankl

CHAPTER NINETEEN

LOOKING TO THE FUTURE

INTERESTS AND ABILITY CHART: To get more insight into your child as he or she gets older, have them complete the following exercise in accordance to the age of the child. The exercise for younger children, pre-school age, would be to bring to their awareness the difference between the categories. Even at a young age, parents can begin to see skills, talents, and interests emerge.

Take a piece of paper, holding it lengthwise, fold it in half, perfectly in half. You then fold it in half again, lengthwise, and you will have four long columns.

And at the top of one column, write **SKILLS**; at the top of the second column, write **EXPERIENCE**; the third, **KNOWLEDGE**; and the fourth, **TALENTS/GIFTS**. (Mentor: Do this for yourself, as well.) It is a fun, enlightening exercise. Abby spent weeks completing hers. The exercise is appropriate for any age level.

DIRECTIONS: in your **SKILL** column, list every skill that you have. Can you type? Can you cook? Can you baby sit? Can you fix a pipe? Can you mow a lawn? Can you write a check? Skills are learnable. Can you walk the dog? Feed the cat? Clean your room? Make your breakfast? Lunch? Tale care of a younger sibling?

You have skills that you might not like using. Are you good at cleaning the house? Yes, but do you want to use that? Yes, it's not that you want to or don't want to use that skill, but you want to put it on your list. Can you train a dog? Do you know how to feed the animals? Can you take care of a younger sibling? List all of your skills in this column whether you enjoy using them or not.

The next column is **EXPERIENCE**. What experiences outside of the home have you had? Have you had a part-time job? Have you done some babysitting? Have you helped teachers in some way? What experiences in life have you had? List those activities that could be considered job-related, whether or not you were paid for your services. Information for this could be found in your "Skills" section. An activity could be a skill and/or an experience.

Next column: What **KNOWLEDGE** do you have? You might not be doing well in school, but when you go home, you read everything you can find about fish. Maybe that's an interest of yours, maybe about fishing, maybe a ham radio, maybe fitness or football or movie stars. People frequently do activities at home about which they don't tell people at school, because they believe their friends may think they're nerdy. What information do you have that most people don't? Abby knows a lot about dieting because she has always been on a diet. She knows a lot about nutrition. She has read any article that she can find on these subjects.

Jim Kwik who wrote *Limitless* was called "the boy with a broken brain" because of an accident in kindergarten, and his "knowledge" is related to improving the brain. He is now a brilliant man who helps others improve their mental acumen.

Abby also knows a lot about how the mind works, only because that subject is of great interest to her, although she has never taught it. Write anything that is of interest to you.

If you were taking a long trip and were buying a magazine to keep your mind occupied, what kind of magazine would you buy? What is your interest in that magazine? You probably won't read every article, but you will read some, which ones? They are indications of what knowledge you have. This is information that you like to know.

The last column, **TALENTS/GIFTS** is the hardest to fill because most people have all been raised not to pat themselves on the back or not to brag. What are your talents and skills? What do you do easily? Abby could not draw a recognizable picture to save her life. If you can, that's a talent. Some of your talents might also be listed in your skill area. Abby could learn the keys of a piano–that would be a skill, but, for her, it would not be a talent. Abby also can read notes of music, which is a skill that she learned as a member of a choir, but she can't carry a tune, so she can't put in her talent column that she's a singer.

Do you work easily with others? Do you get along easily with others? If that's something you're good at, that's a talent. Are you able to help people? Calm them down? That is a talent. Abby's son can fix anything, even as a child. That's a talent. Her daughter can draw or paint beautifully—that, too is a talent.

Do you speak easily in front of others? Are you good on your feet? That's a talent. Do you write particularly well? Some of the students in Abby's Vo-Tech high school drop-out classes were excellent writers. Their grammar may not have been great, but their ability to express themselves on paper was excellent. That's a talent. Writing with perfect grammar is a skill.

To complete the Talent Column, input from family members or close friends is needed. Other people are frequently better at recognizing a child's talents.

Keep this chart for yourself and have your mentees complete this self-analysis. Use it as a way to have them start looking into themselves.

FAVORITE PLACES: Where do they want to live or to work? Do they prefer being indoors or outdoors? Do they like being in a school? Abby loves the smell of a school. She has fond memories of going to and teaching in schools. Her daughter loves the smell of a pool, especially the chlorine, because she's

Gail A. Cassidy

a swimmer. Where do you like being? Or where does the child you are working with like being? Their response tells you a little bit more about them and what they might possibly want to do in the future.

ABILITY TO CHANGE: "How do you want to look, feel, sound?" Abby previously mentioned the young Haitian girl who had only been in America for a year whose parents had very, very heavy accents, and she had none. She wanted to sound American; she wanted to fit in, so she worked with a tape recorder every day until she didn't have an accent." She is a great role model. Abby believes that every child can determine how they look, feel, and sound.

ASK "**What do you want to do every day?**" Do you have any idea what would make you happy if you could do it every day? What kind of relationships do you desire to have with your family and your friends? Family is important, but family is something you don't choose; you choose your friends. If your family is supportive, that's wonderful. If your friends are making you shine, that's wonderful. If your friends are leading you astray, that's not wonderful. Maybe you like them because they accept you, but that doesn't mean they're good for you. And here is where you might conflict with your parents if they are saying don't hang around with "…" They might see your friends from a different perspective. You might want to ask, "How can I help you succeed?"

If, as a parent or teacher who has chosen to be the mentor, referring to your child or your student as a "mentee" may seem awkward. The good news is the term may put your relationship on a different level where the child feels free to be more open in their comments.

In helping kids locate their interests, ask, "What do you feel strongly about? In other words, if you watch the T.V. news, what parts do you not like watching? For example, when there was an oil spill, Abby could not watch the effects on the fish or to the ducks and the birds and the otters. So much life was destroyed because of an oil spill. Abby could not watch it. She can't watch children being hurt in any way. She can't watch war, while her husband, Jake, a former Marine, likes watching true crime stories and war stories.

What do you feel strongly about? That response might give you an idea of what you might want to do in the future and possibly what your mentee might want to do.

ASK: Whom do you admire in life? The important point is why you admire the person you chose. As mentioned previously, Abby used to love Michael Jordan, the basketball player. The why is because of how he handled his fame, how he had made himself an outstanding player even though he was cut from his high school basketball team. Abby admired his determination. She admires Oprah for the same reason, her determination and her impact on people.

After selecting the people they admire, they will find that some characteristic keeps coming up repeatedly. Those characteristics are ones your child admires and therefore may want to have herself. Or possibly your child relates to the person because they do have those same characteristics and feel comfortable because of their similarity. When they start pointing out things that they like in other people, they may be the things that they want to have.

What characteristics do the people they admire have that they share and/or would like to share? What places make them feel good, no matter what their age? Abby mentioned this briefly before. What smells, noises, what feelings do you get? She likes walking into the lobby of a beautiful hotel, probably because she had done so much training in the ballrooms of hotels, and she always loved the ambiance. Some people love the smell of construction and wood being sawed. What places does your child like that makes them feel good?

ASK: What do you enjoy doing in your spare time? Some of the things that kids enjoy they don't tell people about, because they might be laughed at, e.g., catching frogs, building birdhouses. They might laugh at them because they enjoy being on a ham radio contacting people all over the world. What do they do when not watching television, when not on their phone, when not on their computer? When they have nothing to do, what they like to do? It could be baking cookies, planting seeds in a garden, biking, writing. Some people like to write in journals, and writing could be something that they could then make into something greater in the future.

ASK: Which magazines do you read? What articles? What books they choose to read tells about you. As a child Abby read every book she could find on dogs. When she exhausted them, she went to books about cats. Then she went to any book on any animal. Abby loves animals.

ASK: What makes you feel special? What past achievements or honors or recognitions can they recall–a spelling bee they won, a Pinewood Derby car the made, a talk you gave, perfect attendance, a great grade? These achievements could have been given to you by your parents, religious organization, friends, or maybe your school. What have you done that makes you feel good?

ASK: What would your perfect day look like? Where would you live? What town, state, country? Who are your friends? What does your mornings look like? What do you do all day? What time do you get up, go to bed? How do you dress? What is most enjoyable about your perfect day?

ASK: What do you dream or daydream about? If a person cannot sing, they probably do not daydream about being an opera singer. Abby would love to be a singer, but she never daydreams about it because she doesn't have a singing voice that people would enjoy listening to. To daydream about something impossible is unrealistic. Abby used to want to be a ballerina, but she doesn't daydream about it any longer. What anyone dreams or daydreams about could be significant. Would living that daydream make a person happy?

ASK: What would you do if you were a billionaire? According to your child's age, this question may or may not be significant. A better question could be, "If you had unlimited money, what would you do with it?" Your decisions regarding the spending of your money might tell you a little about where you should be going in the future.

Naturally, individuals are most interested in themselves. Psychologists say that in order to love others, we must first love ourselves. By allowing children to "open up" by providing them a safe atmosphere, accepting them, and validating them with enthusiasm, you are accomplishing a great feat. You are making a positive difference in somebody's life, and that will positively affect the lives of others.

EXERCISE:
Make it a point to discuss each of these topics with your child or student, according to what you feel is age appropriate. You could allot one topic a week for discussion.

"Happiness Can Only Exist in Acceptance"

- George Orwell

CHAPTER TWENTY

CONCLUSION

After many years of teaching, Abby Foster finally retired. She had worked hard and spent almost every night of the school year, even school vacations, either correcting papers or creating what she felt were exciting lesson plans for her students.

She wanted her students to succeed and many did, but not everyone did. It was the "not everyone" kids that preyed on her mind. Too many kids seemed unmotivated; some developed an "entitled" attitude; some dropped out of school before graduation.

She wanted to know why. What is the common denominator(s) that determines success or lack of success for students?

Shortly after her retirement, an ad appeared in the paper for a part-time adult school English teacher for high school dropouts, ages 18 to 25. She applied and was immediately hired. She believed that this was the perfect laboratory to study kids who had chosen to drop out of high school. What are the commonalities that caused students to drop out? Are there solutions? Could there be solutions?

If there was anyone at VoTech Adult High School who genuinely cared for her students, it was Abby Foster. She was a dedicated teacher, had gotten great evaluations by her department chairman every year when she taught high school English, and she had great relationships with her peers as well as with the kids in her classes. She loved her job!

Nevertheless, she hurt whenever she lost a student to the streets, to a gang or to a life of poverty, because she knows that a child's chances of success in life are slim once they choose to drop out of school. Many end up in jail; many join gangs.

She saw this job as an opportunity to work at this special adult school for high school dropouts. Maybe she could find a solution - a way to help prevent future dropouts. She truly wanted to make a difference; but, as the semester progressed, she was beginning to doubt herself and her value to the school.

Again, her students were already dropouts. This was their second chance. From her reading of *Winning the Brain Race* by Kearns and Doyle, Abby was particularly aware that in high schools around the country today, there are underachieving, unmotivated students who graduate each year with minimal reading and writing skills. She didn't want her students to have minimal skills.

The fact that America's public schools graduate 700,000 functionally illiterate students every year, and 700,000 more drop out is upsetting to any teacher who cares about her students. Four out of five young adults in a recent survey couldn't summarize the main point of a newspaper article, or read a bus schedule, or figure their change from a restaurant bill, according to the authors.

This year, a number of Abby's students were already failing in spite of the time she devoted to her preparation for class and her individualized work with the students. For such a dedicated teacher, she felt she was not making a difference. Unless something changed dramatically, almost a dozen of her students were not going to graduate with their class.

In her melancholy state of mind, Abby thought to herself, "Maybe it's time for me to move on." "Maybe a solution doesn't exist; maybe I should mind my own business!"

She reminisced about her first year of teaching many decades ago and how she became interested in "disaffected" kids, kids who were bright but just didn't care. As the "newbie" on the staff, she was given what was considered the worst kids, the kids no one wanted to teach, the kids who already had police records, the kids who didn't do homework, pay attention, or even care about school. Her first class was a group of sophomores, average age, 17 instead of the usual sophomore age of 15, and consisted of 28 boys, 2 girls; and they were tough kids!

She recalled how, as the year progressed, she grew to love this roguish group of kids. If they were interested in the topic being taught, she found them to be bright, mischievous, independent, and hard working.

Getting them excited about reading *Silas Marner* and *Julius Caesar* and learning infinitives, gerunds, participles, etc. was easy as long as the material was relevant to them, was fun, and involved no put-downs. Having them help one another was even more rewarding. They learned the material more solidly by helping each another, and they enjoyed the satisfaction of having made a difference in their fellow peers' successes.

Abby's second major encounter with "disaffected" kids came when she was contracted to teach the teachers at a county juvenile detention center. She recalls her shock the day she arrived at the center and discovered the teachers had quit—all of them!

Her revised contract called for her to teach a four-day course, *Success Strategies*, to the teenagers incarcerated at the detention center. "How hard could that be?" she wondered to herself.

The purpose of the course is to teach the teens the importance of choices, attitude, nonverbal communication, and interviewing skills - all done in a fun, fast-paced way.

When Abby was asked if the program was a success, she responded with a resounding NO! And she explained why.

The procedures she had to perform before she even met with the teens should have forewarned her about her upcoming adventure.

After signing in, Abby was directed to the visitor's room with her piles of booklets straining her arms and was asked to remove all of the staples from the two sets of booklets and the plastic spiral binding from another. She was told that the inmates could use these sharp implements for self-mutilation or as weapons. She understood.

With the books readied for the kids, Abby then had to return to her car and stow her purse in the trunk, bringing only a form of ID with her into the building which was then exchanged for a badge. No pencils or pens allowed. Abby's keys were hung at the receptionist's desk.

She was escorted through the metal detector and heavy metal doors, all controlled by the guards in the enclosed glass booth filled with monitors.

The classroom was like any other—desks, blackboard, chairs—nothing unusual, except it was devoid of any decorations, not even chalk. It was stark.

Shortly after they arrived, in marched the first class of boys in line from the shortest to the tallest. Seven young men walked into the room preceded by a large burly guard and followed by two more large men. Seven kids, three guards, two Center employees, my partner and me. Seven adults/seven kids!

Abby had worked with "at risk" kids before, but this experience was different. *Surly, angry, defiant, unresponsive* are the best descriptors that immediately came to mind when she saw the teens. They totally avoided eye contact.

"Please open your books to page 10" evoked looks of disgust, looks that silently screamed, "Don't bother me, Lady?" Abby continued undeterred.

The lightness of the material slowly seeped into the melancholy of a few who actually began to pay attention and almost looked as if they were enjoying the material.

During the discussion of nonverbal communications, Abby asked the class if they were aware that if they see a friend in the hall, their eyebrows briefly flicker upward, then return to their normal position - an involuntary sign of recognition; however, if they see a cute gal they have a crush on, their eyebrows may stay elevated - a sign of interest.

Most seemed to enjoy this information. Abby believes that information was the cause of the most unusual question that took her by surprise. After almost zero response, suddenly a young man thrusts his hand in the air and yells, "Miss, When you were young, were you a hooker?" She detected no disrespect, only curiosity. His classmates did look up to hear her response.

Abby replied, "No, just a teacher." And he seemed fine with that. No one chortled or reacted in a surprised manner at the question.

Abby then showed them how powerful their minds are by holding a ball dangling from a string. She told them that she could "think" it to move. She asked them to tell her the direction they would like the object to move.

She explained that by thinking about the direction of the ball in her mind and moving her eyes in an up-and-down, back-and-forth, or circular position, the tiny muscles in her fingers would unconsciously move the ball. Most people can replicate the experiment. It was merely a demonstration to make the point about the power of their minds.

The downside to this display was the reaction of one of the most vocal boys in the class. Every time Abby called on someone, he would yell, "Don't look in her eyes. She'll control your mind." Initially, she thought he was kidding. He wasn't.

The next day when Abby returned, the same boy demanded, "Why are you back?" She was surprised by his harsh tone.

She said, "I like you guys." Another mistake. He spent the entire period proving how unlikable he is. Finally, Abby gave in and said, "Okay, I don't like you." And he was fine.

He wanted to know where her partner was. Abby explained that she was taking care of her grandchild and would be back on Tuesday. He didn't believe her. He said, "She's never coming back. Teachers don't come back here!"

Now Abby was getting a bit of insight into what was happening. He expected to be let down. He expected people not to like him, and to make sure he was right, he made himself a royal pain in the tush.

And this is why Abby feels the program was not a success. She believes that these kids need someone trained in this material who can work with them every day, not an outsider who first has to gain their trust, and then try to impact this fluid population. They need some stability. They need someone who cares about them.

Abby also slowly learned that in some of her classes, a leader in the class controlled the kids - by a glance, a look, an action that the others immediately understood.

In one class, a very handsome, charismatic young man was an absolute sweetheart. He loved everything Abby presented, was totally cooperative, and sweet-talked the daylights out of her, and she bought in – hook, line, and sinker – until she finally saw the surreptitious "look." The "look" he furtively shot at his classmates if

186

they were doing something – like participating – that he didn't want them to be doing, and the look was responded to immediately. For example, if Abby said, "Turn to page 45," she finally realized that no one touched his book until Mr. Sweet-talk touched his.

One day Abby asked one of the guards if he ever became attached to any the kids. He responded very strongly, "Not anymore!" He explained that early on he had become attached to some of the kids and gotten "burned." He wouldn't explain further.

Some of the kids did touch Abby's heart; some were scary; some so defiant that they made teaching very difficult.

The guard explained that these kids are "players," street-smart kids who have mastered the art of manipulation. He added that those who aren't players are either brain-fried or illiterate. "That's why they don't open the book when you tell them to. They can't read." Abby hadn't thought about that.

She also asked the guard why the kids were here. He replied, "Murder, rape, drugs, armed robbery." Wow!

Does Abby believe these kids are throwaways, impossible to save? She does believe that those who have permanent brain damage will probably spend the rest of their lives in a protected area, or perhaps it should be said, "hopefully spend their lives confined in some way," because they can kill and maim and not really be responsible because of their diminished capacity.

The extremes are the brain-fried and the manipulators. If Abby compares them to a barrel of fruit, she would say there are some rotten apples, i.e., throwaways; and there are ones on the verge of turning sour, that, if taken under a strong caring person's wing, could turn out to be effective members of society.

Abby is very aware of the numbers. According to some experts, we are failing almost half of the teenage population who either drop out, graduate as illiterates, or develop an attitude of "entitlement." To prevent too many apples from rotting, she believes teachers have to help out in the field—they have to nurture the crop.

Hearing her kids about to enter her classroom, Abby snaps out of her reverie as she watches the students take their seats.

With a start, she thinks, "I wonder if what I learned from my first class decades ago and from my Juvenile Detention kids would apply to today's kids?"

"The world is different today," she knows. "Technology, transportation, entertainment, even foods have changed," she realizes as she sees her class settle in, take their books out, and stow their phones where they cannot be seen.

Then it struck her: "What has not changed over the years is human nature. A Theory of Human Motivation by American psychologist Abraham Maslow is still a highly regarded source of information for determining human needs. His Hierarchy of Needs is still in effect: 1) Survival Needs (food, water, clean air, and shelter), 2) Safety Needs (mental and physical), 3) Social Needs (people: friends, and family), 4) Esteem Needs (acceptance, validation, self-belief), all leading to 5) Self-Actualization (making a difference in the world).

All five areas are as relevant today as they were when Maslow wrote about them in 1943.

With a tingle of giddiness and a feeling of hope, Abby begins her class and enjoys the feelings of excitement and promise build as she interacts with her students.

She knows what she has to do!

With only a few months left before graduation, Abby decides to confront the problem head on. She will personally study, interview, and write a case study for each "at risk" student in order to determine what their mindset is and what their intentions are insofar as graduating with their class. She hopes she will learn something that she could use in the future. Even more, she hopes she can keep these kids in school so they can graduate.

But first, she has something she intends to do in order to make the interview meaningful and not rote. She wants to make sure that each student is aware of her recognition of what is special about them, that this is not a meaningless prying into their psyches.

She challenges herself to write a brief case study about each student that concerns her. The format is always the same: what she sees as positives about their personality or abilities or attitude or interaction with classmates - anything that she regards as a plus.

At the end of the case study, she decides to include an area of recommendation, something that would benefit the student in the long run.

Because of time constraints, Abby limits her case studies to those kids she feels are at risk of dropping out or failing out of school. Not being a neighborhood school, most of the students don't hang out or even live near one another. If, perchance, a student feels "left out" because they didn't get a case study written about them, she will make the time to include them.

All interviews are done outside the classroom and are not shared with their classmates.

Before the interviews with the students begin, Abby studies the personalities in her class and writes "general impressions" case studies on those students who are the most challenging.

Her intent is to find commonalities, positive traits and conditions to build on. She keeps in mind questions such as

1. Is there anything, words and/or deeds, that all people respond to?
2. What, if any, commonalities are there regarding interacting with students?
3. What actions can students (or anyone) adopt to feel better about themselves and/or others?
4. What human relation skills should everyone adopt?
5. What's the importance of non-verbal communication?
6. How important is listening?
7. Which ethics are most important to adopt?
8. Does everyone have to adopt the same ethic?
9. What part does belief play in a person's behavior, actions and reactions?
10. Besides Shelter and Safety, what's the most important thing(s) a person needs to succeed in life?

As a result of her interviews and case studies, Abby has come up with a list of what she referred to as The Laws of Human Nature which include the principles of S (Safety) - A (Acceptance) - V (Validation) - and (E (Enthusiasm).

For a free copy of Abby's book on Basic Human Laws (Code of Ethics) resulting from her years of teaching English to high school dropouts, ages 18 to 25, go to https://www.cassidycourses.com/ SelfEsteem.

Abby is very aware that our current turbulent times are affecting everyone in different ways. We live in stressful times, times that may make us question our own values, question our own worth. That's why outside validation is so vitally important to children. She believes that parents and/or teachers are the great potential source of that validation.

Her recipe of equal parts Safety, Acceptance, Validation, and Enthusiasm will provide CONFIDENT, happy kids.

From the *Speaking for Teens* class, read more testimonials, using the S-A-V-E recipe. Check them out. The entire 19 pages can be found at https://bit.ly/2Mkflgc.

Another option is to visit https://www.cassidycourses.com and learn about the three programs already fully developed. Each course provides acceptance and validation for every participant. A brief video precedes each lesson explaining what should be covered. Each lesson also contains videos for every class, downloadable information for the students, and a script for the session. All of the work has been done in order to facilitate the training.

Either way, Abby would be delighted if you shared in her belief that a strong self-concept is essential to the success of any person. "What the mind can conceive and believe, it can achieve." -Napoleon Hill; but first a person has to believe in him- or herself.

Abby believes that every child can experience a high level of self-esteem, which, of course, leads to self-actualization, the top of Maslow's Hierarchy of Needs.

Abby believes that people, especially kids, can live their own framework of beliefs, guiding principles when they believe in themselves. They can then ask: What is my personal role in the world?

Helen Keller said, "The only thing worse than being blind is having sight but no vision." These courses provide the vision, the self-belief, and the confidence to pursue their goals.

Henry Thoreau said, "Go confidently in the direction of your dreams. Live the life you have imagined." This, of course, is possible if a person believes in himself and his or her ability to do so.

Helping kids believe in themselves is the greatest gift we can give them. As we believe, so we are.

Thanks for reading,
Abby Foster

P.S. Join our mailing list, https://www.cassidycourses.com.

The greatest gift
that you can give to
others is the gift of
unconditional love
and acceptance.

- Brian Tracy